AN ESSENTIAL GUIDE TO
ASCENSION

LIVING IN THE FIFTH DIMENSION

TERESA BROWN

Copyright 2023 Teresa Brown

All rights reserved, including the right to reproduce this book, or portions thereof in any form. No part of this text may be reproduced, transmitted, downloaded, decompiled, reverse engineered, or stored in any form or introduced into any information storage and retrieval system, in any form or by any means, whether electronic or mechanical without the express permission of the author.

Disclaimer: The information in this book is not intended to be treated as a substitute for professional medical advice. Any use of information in this book is at the reader's discretion. Neither the author or the publisher can be held responsible for any loss, claim or damage arising out of the use, or misuse, of the suggestions and techniques. The views expressed in this work are solely those of the author.

ISBN: 9798865633471

A practical fact-based guide to ascension

Explaining the present chaos
& future possibilities

Contents

Part One: The Present Moment is Crucial
    The Present Moment
    A Crucial Moment in Time
    The 2012 Phenomenon
    The Threat of Free Thinking
    What Are The Alternatives
    The Collective Consciousness
    The Collective Consciousness Project
    Manifestation and the Maharishi Effect
    Competition or Cooperation
    Retaining Essential Freedom
    An Auspicious Moment in Time
    The Microcosm and Macrocosm
    HeartMath Institute
    Experiencing Heart-based Consciousness
    A Blue-Print for Mother Earth
    The Power is Within
    The Great Illusion
    Question Everything
    The Significance of the Present Moment

Part Two: Past Deceptions and Hidden Truth
    The Realm of Limitation
    The Great Connection

Leylines
Ancient Civilisations
Old Science - New Revelations
Sunken Cities & The Bermuda Triangle
How and Why Earth Shifts Occur
Standing Stones & Astronomy
Inter-Galactic Intervention

Part Three: The Process of Ascension
Accessing the Higher Dimensions Future Possibilities
Accessing The Higher Realms
The Process of Ascension
Inner Alchemy
Identifying Old Traits & Releasing the Past
Celestial Chakras & the Merkabah Frequency
Our Awakening & Astral Travel
Creative Visualisation & Heart Mind Harmony
The Merkabah & Sacred Geometry
The Mysterious Human DNA
Our Sovereign Heritage
Hyper-Communication
Releasing the Past & Purifying the Present
Activating Crystalline DNA
Coping with Energy Shifts
Creating the New Paradigm

Introduction

At this present moment, humanity is experiencing change at a rate so rapid it has never been witnessed before.

This rapid change is in all areas, not just technology.

We are living at a time when mass extinction of species, is evident. Global warming threatens the environment. Social control is being tightened on a global scale. Events that were once the making of science fiction movies, have become reality in the blink of an eye.

What are we to make of these cataclysmic situations? Are we to simply sleepwalk through the next few years with our fingers crossed hoping for salvation?

This book uses scientific evidence alongside ancient spiritual teachings to offer simple, and effective explanations as to why these events are occurring. It also offers constructive ideas as to what we can do both individually and collectively to ensure a positive outcome.

How can we be so sure that we are actually on the cusp of seismic change? Change that is seismic in all meanings of the word: geological change involving the Earth, and also change of enormous proportions, effecting all areas of life.

How can we, as an intelligent species, be so sure that we are currently going through the predicted resurrection and ascension that so many spiritual texts have foretold?

What changes will need to be made to make society work for us and for the planet?

Can humanity avoid catastrophic conflict and self-destruction?

Will we all make it through? Or will some of us sleepwalk into oblivion?

These are some of the many questions that we will endeavour to address as we venture through ancient writings and long held beliefs.

Science, Economics, History and Ancient Esoteric Teachings will be there at our side with hard evidence as we explore the answers and solutions to these intriguing questions.

Part One

The Present Moment is Crucial!

The Present Moment
A Crucial Moment in Time
The 2012 Phenomenon
The Threat of Free Thinking
What Are The Alternatives
The Collective Consciousness
The Collective Consciousness Project
Manifestation and the Maharishi Effect
Competition or Cooperation
Retaining Essential Freedom
An Auspicious Moment in Time
The Microcosm and Macrocosm
HeartMath Institute
Experiencing Heart-based Consciousness
A Blue-Print for Mother Earth
The Power is Within
The Great Illusion
Question Everything
The Significance of the Present Moment

The Present Moment

Everything is in a constant state of change. Nothing is permanent. The present moment is all there is, and the current situations, that we are experiencing globally, are of great significance. The timing and importance of our action has never been more crucial.

Profound changes are occurring on many levels: in our thinking, in our society, in our community, on our planet and in our galaxy and beyond. And they are all occurring now.

Everything is in a continual state of perpetual impermanence and change.

It is our responsibility to collectively ensure that all change is for the greatest good of all, and not for a small, greedy, self-serving minority.

It is our responsibility to ensure that basic freedoms and human rights are not only preserved and strengthened, but also placed at the very centre of our civilisation going forwards.

We are presently witnessing first hand, major shifts in society as we have known it. We have globally experienced government coercion, and control on a previously unprecedented scale. The Collective Consciousness of humanity has been shaken to its very core by an onslaught of exaggerated and unrealistic fears.

This has caused the tangible frequency of panic and anxiety to resonate throughout humanity, adversely affecting our most vulnerable and impressionable, and of course, our children too.

The content of this book is non-political, non-judgemental and non-denominational.

This book does not seek to divide, but to combine and unite, in truth, and compassion. By presenting a fact-based analogy of the past, present and future, readers will be inspired to simply take back control and to build a positive foundation for humanity going forwards.

History often asks the question: "How do dictators and oppressive regimes gain control?" We have probably all heard the same answer: "It is when good, honest people stand by and do nothing."

What we are witnessing now, in this very moment in time, is delusion in all areas of society. We are witnessing the continued rise of an oppressive, restrictive "global elite" who are in a state of delusion, believing they have a right to control others, and that they also have right to obscene wealth.

On the flip side, we have the masses, which accounts for most of us. And the masses are deluded to. Trapped in the delusion that they are powerless, tied by false limitations that do not really exist.

Where, when and how will this delusion end? Most people are fed a diet of fear, shame and distrust from the news media, which is currently owned by a handful of the deluded super rich.

Every corrupt negative news story, and every unjust restriction enforced upon us, will simply encourage us to wake up, and to respond accordingly.

Enough is enough.

We can already see the curtailment of our basic human rights occurring before our very eyes. We can feel the narrative from the global media inciting division, victimising and blaming the innocent and vulnerable as scapegoats, whilst despicable acts of corporate greed and devastating ecocide go unannounced, and unpunished.

We are also only all too aware that social services and health care, once freely available are now simply no longer in existence or have been heavily regulated and privatised. We are all experiencing coercion to participate in an, as yet unregulated, and untested drug trial, whilst signing away any and all rights of compensation and redress.

We are, by our very nature, wired to be trusting and caring individuals. We are social beings who have survived over centuries by cooperation and compassion. These virtues are currently being undermined and manipulated.

We live in an age when **not** everything we read is truth. Main stream media has managed to consign virtually any form of free thinking to the festering heap of 'conspiracy theory'.

If a new idea seems feasible, and we follow it on social media, or repeat it to our friends and family, we also run the risk of being labelled and ridiculed as a co-conspirator, a believer in conspiracy theories. We are made to feel like unworthy extremists with radical outrageous beliefs, as if we were members of an undesirable cult.

And so we learn to remain silent.
We learn to remain comfortable in conformity.
Conforming to the norm.
The norm of social obedience.

We are living at a time when we can read a legitimate news article in one broadsheet and see the same news completely reversed in another. We can see the TV News media broadcast a story with one spin on it, and see it refuted and altered on another channel.

Misinformation: false, inaccurate information which is deliberately intended to deceive.

This has been particularly evident with the recent Covid19 pandemic. For example photographs of hospital wards claiming to be from one country have been broadcast, and the same photo being used by another news agency claiming to be from somewhere else entirely.

Facts, figures and data have all been subject to mis-interpretation and mis-information.

The all important camera angle can swing the news story and its content. We can all remember the statistics of high attendance at various political rallies during the election campaigns, and the accompanying photographs of vast crowds of people.

These figures later to be disputed, and backed up by realistic images taken with a camera using a wider long-shot lens, evidencing the poor attendance. Media manipulation!

Recently the largest convoy of trucks ever assembled anywhere in the world rendezvoused in Ottawa, Canada to demand freedom from oppressive government mandates. And fellow sympathisers were participating all over the globe, none of it was reported by the mainstream media. There were protests on a massive scale throughout UK and Europe, through Asia, New Zealand and Australia.

Known as the Freedom Convoy 2022, it was not streamed live by any media news channel, anywhere. It was not reported in any newspapers or acknowledged for what it was anywhere other than the social media videos and memes posted by the protestors themselves.

These social media posts were rapidly censored and removed by various social media platforms, as usual, but the sheer volume of participants kept the movement and it's demands in the public domain.

Although the main social media platforms removed posts and articles pertaining to the Freedom Convoy Movement, they were not able to dissuade the peaceful protest as it was massive!

Their actions effectively resulted in a huge shift in the collective consciousness.

It was a shift in the right direction. It was the inevitable shift towards compassion, peace and co-operation.

The global establishment began rapidly backing down. They began back-tracking on their former strategy to impose even more restrictions and mandates. They began quickly lifting formerly imposed restrictions and changing their fear-based narrative.

Unsurprisingly the mass media and governments did not credit the Freedom Convoy 2022 movement with having effected positive change, but used other narratives instead, to introduce the easing of the mandates that had for the past two years, violated basic Human Rights.

Many trusted government leaders tried to instil fear and panic by portraying the peaceful protestors as radical racists, or angry, armed militia.

Fortunately the Freedom Convoy 2022 organisers were well aware of the use, in the past, of highly paid saboteurs. The organisers advised members to keep their mobile phones handy and to constantly film what was occurring, particularly anyone carrying controversial political signs, or anyone instigating violence.

Some mainstream news broadcasts later referred to the convoy as being 'dangerous armed agitators,' and 'stealing food from the homeless.'

In fact, nothing was further from the truth.

We simply must question everything.

If something so obviously peaceful and well-intentioned was not reported globally as it occurred, what else has been manipulated over the years, to keep us all subdued, fearful, divided and confused.

Fake news is the new war cry!

To decipher what is fake, we must also decipher what is truth!

In our efforts to search for the truth we are being fed a deliberate diet of deceit.

A Crucial Moment in Time

Never before in the history of modern humanity have we had access to so much information at the tip of our fingers. At the tap of key or an app, we can access so much data. Yet this information needs to be constantly validated and fact checked as so much of it is false. So much information is, in fact, posted to create distraction, fear and panic.

It would appear that the overall agenda of our global governments is to confuse us, to distract and divide us. What might their reasoning for doing this be?

Can we ever find justice a world where the rules have apparently been made over hundreds of decades by self-serving sociopaths with little or no conscience?

Isn't it time we are now able to chose empathy and compassion over greed and avarice?

If we, as an intelligent species, are to survive beyond this era of desperate division, we must adopt new compassionate lifestyles, and adapt to an ever fluctuating evolving environment.

For too long mankind has gone against Nature. The Industrial Revolution redesigned a society that had previously worked the land and flowed with its seasonal changes. We have seen so many injustices carried out in the name of profit, capital gain, and so called success.

All over the globe, free people have been enslaved and colonised in the name of 'civilisation' and 'religion'.

At the time these outrageous atrocities took place, the ruling elite made sure that the main body of society believed this was in the best interests of all concerned. The persecution of indigenous populations in the Americas, in Africa, India and Australia, China, Asia, virtually everywhere, was carried out under the umbrella of 'civilisation'.

Society was convinced by the governing body of the day that "… savages and 'child-like' lesser beings needed to be civilised…." Today we rightly question and abhor these underhanded tactics. Yet they are still being deployed today.

Under our very noses, the same tactics are being used to set our society against refugees seeking asylum. We are constantly being fed a diet of hatred and division. The mainstream media sets out to stir up the fear of refugees flooding into the country, taking over our towns and cities. They do this by demeaning their target, by making them appear as lesser beings, then the powers that be, aim to divide opinion and instil derision and fear.

We have seen this happen on numerous occasions, with homeless people, single mothers, people of colour, people with different religious beliefs or different sexual identities. This system of division and control is tired, broken and outdated.

If we are to survive as a species we must seek to expand our conscious awareness and in so doing, lift the Collective Consciousness of all humanity out of the gutter of greed.

How do we know we are able to do this? And furthermore how do we set about lifting Consciousness in ourselves and in others?

Life has a pattern, a sequence. Just as the seasons ebb and flow, just as the sun sets and rises, there are patterns and sequences on a far larger scale. There are larger natural cycles that exist, that have a profound affect upon the interplay of life itself.

The 2012 Phenomenon

The year 2012 held a secret of great significance. There was much excitement about the year 2012 as it was the end date of the ancient Mayan calendar.

The Mayan Long Count calendar is cyclical, it began on August 11th 3114 BC centuries before the Mayan culture even existed! It ended on 21st December 2012, centuries after the Mayan culture had ceased to thrive.

What did our ancestors understand that we have now forgotten? What messages were they leaving for us to decipher?

The ending of the Mayan Calendar was publicised by the mass media with the usual fear-mongering. Scholars now look back at this event that became known as The 2012 Phenomenon.

The 2012 Phenomenon consists of a range of beliefs that a series of cataclysmic events would occur on or around 21st December 2012, because of the imminent end of the Mayan Long Count Calendar. The secrets that this Long Count Calendar revealed and recorded was in fact the existence of a long-ranging recurring cycle of approximately 5,125 years.

Rather than experiencing armageddon, and the end of the world as we know it, instead humanity witnessed a seismic shift in Consciousness.

All the major planets, Pluto, Uranus, Neptune, Saturn, Mars, Venus and Jupiter, our Earth and Moon, Venus and Mercury, all fell into alignment, with the Sun. The Sun also began a new Solar Maximum. At exactly the same time The Dog Star, Sirius, completed its orbit around the Milky Way. At the same time Scientists discovered that the centre of our galaxy was, in fact, a massive Black Hole. An awesome and exciting series of astrological events and discoveries!

Yet the greatest excitement of 2012 was the celebration of the re-discovery of The Great Cycle of 5,125 years that the Long Count Calendar brought to our attention.

This cycle is significant in so far as it marked a reset not a finality. It marked a rebirth not a death. The birth of a new age and a new great astrological cycle officially began on 21st December 2012.

However, as with all things in nature, everything flows according at its allotted pace and towards its allotted purpose. There is only impermanence and change. And the roots of this particular new epoch of change began to stir back in the 1960's.

The unfurling birth of the new frequencies of the Age of Aquarius were first expressed by the grass-root movements of the 1960's. During this decade the Collective Consciousness of the younger generation expanded and we witnessed radial social movements that challenged convention.

The 1960's was the decade that saw old outdated social etiquette tossed aside in a global wave of awakening that embraced individuality, self-expression, and unconditional love. New psychedelic drugs were the fashion of the day and were openly taken by those in the public eye.

The global elite and global governments became alarmingly aware that this new generation posed a new and very serious threat.

The Threat of Free Thinking

As their mindsets were blown open to other dimensions, by the use of the mind-altering substances, the new generation saw through the fallacies of the denser reality. The sudden beauty and blissful experiences that the '60's psychedelics revealed to their users, meant that the younger generation now had a unique insight into realms so awesome and so all embracing, that the horrors of war, famine, hatred and control, became totally abhorrent to them.

The generations just a few years prior to this, in the '40's and '50's had been indoctrinated through the horrors of two global World Wars and a catastrophic global financial depression, to obey without question.

At that time despair, rationing, conscription, and death on a daily basis, were the fears complicit in conditioning an entire populace on a global scale.

Enter the era of the Hippie, love, peace and above all free thinking and free expression.

The Beatles publicised the philosophies of Indian Guru's. Cassius Clay became Muhammad Ali and refused to be drafted into the Vietnam war. Every day folk grew their hair longer, and felt freer to follow their own expression of fashion, music, speech and work. The old order was shocked. The old ways were washed with wonder as the tide began to turn and alter old social norms forever. Peacefully. Gently. Effectively.

This generation of peace-loving pioneers, are currently the grandparents of today. Their revolutionary values shifted collective awareness and helped society to accept that radical counter-culture pioneers positive changes. Greater demands for individual freedom and for peace on a global scale could not simply be ignored by those in authority.

Despite the efforts of the politicians and global elite, to instil fear with the "cold war", the West versus Russia, and the missile crises with Cuba, and the war in Vietnam; despite all these tactics, the rainbow peace signs grew in number, painted on colourful campers, and worn on the garments of the radical new thinkers.

Through faith and persistence their cause became the truth. Their philosophy became ingrained in the hearts and minds of humanity. The Collective Consciousness shifted.

The Greenham Common Women's Peace Camp, and other anti war movements followed into the 1980's and 1990's. Racial Equality, Gay Rights, Women's Liberation, Animal Rights, were all seeds from the same fruit. The fruit of a growing new Collective Consciousness.

Throughout the 1990's a growing trend emerged labelled the New Age movement. We witnessed groups of New Age Travellers, free spirits seeking an alternative way of life, more at peace with nature, more harmonious with life itself. Peaceful, non-violent groups emerged exposing corporate greed and the violation of the environment for capital gain and profit.

The large burger giant McDonalds was the subject of much exposure for their devastation of the Brazilian rainforest.

Other groups of peaceful New Age protestors occupied treetops to prevent the decimation of ancient woodlands to build the Newbury Bypass.

As relatively harmless as these protests were, we now know that the UK police carried out covert undercover operations to infiltrate these groups. Some of the undercover policemen even went so far as to have deep personal relationships with some of the protestors. Some of these unscrupulous covert cops even fathered children with their unsuspecting long-term lovers. What depths the dark agenda is prepared to stoop to? How cruel and demeaning their schemes are when exposed in the full light of day.

No surprise then, when the next group of truth-seekers and freedom-lovers emerged: Anonymous. This group was not going to be quite so easily humiliated and controlled. Having no known leaders, no geographical office, no agenda, just fast and effective collective action organised through social media.

We can see that the tide of change constantly adjusts in order to reveal truth and expose deceit. The waves of social change, of collective awakening and true democratic justice are inevitably gaining more credibility and support. The old order is diminishing.

Although Anonymous was fractured as the social media platforms tightened their controls, they were the first cyber-based global organisation, and they were a true force for positive change. As regulations were applied the social media site 'Twitter' became a mediocre platform of trivia and little else. Facebook and Instagram became more restricted and establishment-based. We are still witnessing more and more unfair and unwarranted censorship as each day dawns.

We have seen Wikileaks, and the release of 'classified' records and documents, and we have seen the power of the internet in action during campaigns like Black Lives Matter and the MeToo campaigns.

And so we fast forward to the present decade, the 2020's, and we arrive at time where we can clearly see that those in control, those who play a part in the old order, are desperately trying to hang on to the familiar fears and distractions as a means of control and division. We can also see those controls being far less effective. The control by fear, the control by separation and division, the control by untruth after untruth, is now being exposed for what it is. Untruth.

Society is at this very moment transitioning into a new state of play. We are threatened with the greatest global financial recession in history. We are threatened with climate change, fires raging from California to Australia. Ice caps melting, and species extinction at a rate unprecedented. We are threatened with the collapse of freedoms as we knew them due to an unseen enemy.

The unseen enemy has been many things. At first, during the psychedelic sixties, it was the War on Drugs. This morphed into the War on Want, and then the War against Terror. Now we have experienced the War against a Virus. We've had the opportunity to rehearse this particular type of war with other viruses such as AIDS, SARS, Dengue fever, Ebola, and then it was the classic turn of Covid-19.

The Governments issued rule change, after rule change and we witnessed the general population, once again, becoming tired, listless, and suspicious. Lateral Flow Tests were proven to have been inconclusive and to have a high inaccuracy or failure rate.

There is the additional fear-based element of enforced vaccination. We witnessed the unprecedented action of doctors and care-workers loosing their jobs if they wished to exert the basic human right of choice over their own body.

We experienced the forced introduction of vaccination passports, which went hand in hand with the curtailment of freedom of speech, protest, and free movement.

More division, more fear, more coercion. The parallel precedent of the Nazi regime in Germany, and their programme of eugenics is concerning.

Whatever we find ourselves facing today, we are torn between belief and distrust.

Are we "conspiracy theorists" or are we fervent followers of the government and mass media?

What a choice!

Caught between a rock and a hard place!

Fortunately there are alternatives.

What Are The Alternatives?

When we connect with our consciousness, our higher state of awareness, we discover a calmness, a frequency that resonates with peace, love, harmony and most of all truth.

When we go within, through meditation, (or begin by simply letting go and day dreaming), we find a space where truth resides. Our heart-based consciousness resonates with truth.

What is consciousness?
What is this essence that dwells within us and beyond us?

Our consciousness is, in fact, everything; everything in the past, everything in the present moment and everything and every possibility in the future. It is our inner self, our higher self, and it is also connected to everyone everywhere. How can this be?

As we read the words above, let us begin to consider; 'Who or what is reading this? Who or what is making sense of the words that are on this paper? Who or what is deciphering and decoding the symbols written here and speaking them internally into our inner most thought?'

Just take a moment two to ponder; 'Who or what is the thinker behind the thought?'

The thinker.

The "I am".

This is our consciousness.

This is awareness of self.

Later we explore the activation of Crystalline DNA and the significant role this heart-based consciousness plays in the Ascension process.

We maybe familiar with the term 'subconscious', which scientists understand to be approximately 95% or more of our entire thought process. The subconscious is often likened to functioning rather like a computer hard drive, since it accepts information without judgement and stores it. It has no rational discriminating facility and does not decipher fact from fiction. This is why we often feel emotionally involved when watching a movie or reading a book.

Our subconscious learns by repetition and rote. It is that mysterious part of ourselves that can safely take control of the driving while we slip off into a daze thinking about what we're going to eat for dinner! It's the part of us that can multi-task allowing us to safely function on different levels of awareness, on different levels of consciousness.

The Collective Consciousness

The Collective Consciousness is the body of thought energy that holds society together.

Like everything else on the planet, it is susceptible to perpetual impermanence and change. Take for example the new shopping trend "Black Friday'". This once unheard of terminology has recently become engrained into the Collective Consciousness. It has become a tangible reality. Advertisers use it with gusto every November. It has become an accepted cultural pattern. The Collective Consciousness has expanded and altered.

There are more subtle examples of how thought, particularly collective thought, has changed society. Successful changes in our social norms have always begun from grass-root level.

History has evidenced this.

We are all aware of the social changes that have been effected on present day society from group-held thoughts on war, animal rights, equal opportunities etc.,.

The innate power of our thoughts, is little understood and taught. And for a good reason!

The power of our thoughts can alter the physical world.

(We explore techniques for this later in this book!)

We have the ability to create and manifest by enhancing our thought energy. We all have the essential ability to create our reality. We are just constantly prevented and discouraged from doing so!

We know this to be a fact by referring to the Collective Consciousness Project.

The Collective Consciousness Project

The phenomenon of mass emotional-thought energy has been seriously studied by scientists and engineers since 1998.

This ongoing project is called the Collective Consciousness Project. It is a long-term experiment to identify an unconscious worldwide connection between humans, as they experience similar emotions.

Scientists are actively measuring responses from global events on a daily basis. In particular they monitor global tragedies like the 9/11 twin towers disaster and the tragic death of Diana Princess of Wales.

Whilst research is ongoing, there is conclusive evidence that proves the existence of the phenomenon of collective consciousness, that is accessible through the individual human psyche. The energy from the collective consciousness has been proven to have a direct effect, be that negative or positive, on how society functions.

This project is an international, multidisciplinary collaboration of scientist and engineers who collect data continuously. Their purpose is to examine subtle correlations that reflect the activity of consciousness in the world. It has been proven by this study that large scale group consciousness effects the physical world.

Collective Consciousness is the belief-based thought-energy that bonds society together.

The phenomenon of the shared set of beliefs, values and ideas that flow through society make up Collective Consciousness. It is the energy of our combined beliefs, customs and attitudes.

For example a previously held aspect of the Collective Consciousness was that it was a sin to live together without marriage, and a further sin to bear a child outside wedlock. These particular long-held concepts have been subjected to change. However long-held they may have been, they were still impermanent. They had to change, because the frequency of the Collective Consciousness had altered.

It is the frequency of the Collective Consciousness that holds society together. The mass media are currently desperately manipulating that vital core energy frequency.

The global mass media are controlled by governments and a handful of extraordinarily rich billionaires. A certain Australian based individual proudly boasts that his news corporation can control who the next British Prime Minister will be. How crazy is that? He is so sure of the efficacy of his media mind manipulation that he openly brags about it!

Giant tech companies are also in on the action. Censorship and control of our social media posts is the new norm now. We seem to be rendered powerless in the face of their power, wealth and global reach.

And yet we have in fact never been more powerful! We simply need to remember how powerful we actually are, where that power resides and how to activate it!

We are masters of manifestation.

Manifestation and 'The Maharishi Effect'

We have the ability to co-create our reality. Every thought, word and action influences the collective consciousness. It is this body of energy that creates the structure to the matrix of material energy in which we all exist.

Science has even calculated the amount of energy that is required to create the momentum for change. It is surprisingly infinitesimal. Merely the square root of 1% is required to influence the process of a change in the collective consciousness. Unsurprising then that our opinions and freedoms are closely monitored!

This percentage of energy that effects the unified field of the matrix in which we exist, is known as 'The Maharishi Effect.' It dates back to the 1980's when the benefits of group transcendental meditation were measured by scientists. In the vicinity of the many cities where the group meditations took place, it was noted that crime rates began to fall, domestic violence rate dropped, truancy at school and work were lowered too. Scientists calculated the change on the population compared to the group numbers and the figure of the square root of 1% was derived.

The current population of the world is 7.8 billion, so it follows that 1% is 78 million, the square root of which is a mere 8,832 people. This is the minimum global figure required to effect the momentum for change!

In the distant past, Buddhist monks held a sacred space by chanting for peace, in their consecrated temples in the

Himalayan mountain tops. Sadly many have now been displaced and scattered, by oppressive political parties, and forced to live in exile around the globe.

It is our individual responsibility to now hold that sacred frequency within ourselves. As we seek enlightenment for ourselves, so we illuminate those close to us, and connect with other like-minded souls globally. Everything is energy, and like attracts like.

When our own individual consciousness becomes still and calm, it's frequency becomes attuned to, and identified with the unified field of energy that resonates with all the laws of nature, and the laws of creation.

The key to effective change is stillness. The key to effective change is the ability to resonate on the heart-based consciousness, in harmony with the virtues of unconditional love and peace.

Once again, it is unsurprising that we are being deliberately kept in a constant state of fear, comparison and division. We are conditioned to distance as far as possible from the virtues of love and peace, and to even fear or ridicule the notions of love and peace!

Our true collective conscious, given the opportunity, will create Utopia, a heaven here on Earth.

Competition or Co-operation

We have already identified the fact that we have experienced the end of an astrological cycle of 2,125 years. This was an epoch dominated by conflict, cruelty and control.

During the final 100 years of that long cycle, the Twentieth Century, modern science exerted a great influence on our technological inventions, and also on our way of thinking.

New scientific thought taught us that life evolved based on the theory of the 'survival of the fittest.' This philosophy, was expounded in 1869, by Charles Darwin's publication "The Origin of the Species'.

This philosophy wad based on the belief that through conflict, competition and control the strongest of the species, those that fought to dominate their environment, were the most likely to be successful in surviving and reproducing.

The idea of survival by 'out-competing' for limited resources was also applied to the Human race.

Competition and comparison became engrained in the collective consciousness. Seeds of division, pitched mankind against itself.

History has once again, evidenced how oppressive regimes, and extremists from various religious and political groups, turned to science to try and sanction racial superiority. The science of eugenics, of selective breeding, is an off-shoot from the theory first expounded by Darwin in his publication 'The Origin of the Species.'

The supposition of the survival of the fittest, is poorly conceived and misleading. It is now being questioned as the collective consciousness shifts and changes. We are now becoming aware of new studies that prove beyond doubt that nature survives through co-operation, not conflict and control.

Nature survives through co-operation, we can see this every which way we turn.

Scientists have now become aware that trees communicate with each other through underground wires made of a living fungus that transmits antibodies and information between tree species.

We know that animals thrive and survive by removing parasites from each other. Ants build nests and live communally, continually helping and assisting each other. Plants co-evolve with birds to spread their seed. Everywhere we look we witness co-operation and co-existence.

We know that nature survives and thrives on nurturing each and every aspect of life as the interplay is one of dependancy each on one another. Our own body, for example, is composed of trillions of cells working as a cohesive unit. We are effectively a collaboration of trillions of cells working together to form tissues, and organs. And these cells co-operate with thousands bacteria that inhabit our skin and intestines, assisting us in digesting the food we eat, or combatting external pathogens.

Everything co-operates in Nature. Plants, for example, produce oxygen through photosynthesis. Without plants, we would not be able to even breathe!

We have everything to gain by favouring co-operation over competition. Can we now, at last, devise a lifestyle that flows in harmony with all life on Earth?

We are here at an auspicious and critical time. We desperately need to master technology and not allow it to master the human species. We desperately need to retain the freedoms that our ancestors enjoyed. The freedom of being an essential part of, and at one with, Nature, with Mother Earth. The freedom of being at one with the ever changing continuity of the seasonal shifts. The freedom of being at one with the ebb and flow of the Great Mystery that is life.

We are here at this auspicious and critical time as a new astrological golden age emerges. It is imperative we retain our essential human-ness.

Retaining Essential Freedom

The progress of Artificial Intelligence (A.I.) has been rapid and now has the alarming ability to easily transcend biology and seriously threaten the future of humanity.

This is often referred to as The Singularity, an hypothesis when Artificial Intelligence (A.I.) due to rapid technological growth, becomes uncontrollable and irreversible, resulting in unimaginable changes to humans and other carbon-based life forms, which when assessed by A.I. are simply classified as an inefficient waste of space.

A recent study for the McKinsey Global Institute assessed that A.I. could presently replace up to thirty percent of the current human labour force. During the past ten years robots have become increasingly self-aware. Robots have passed cognitive tests such as recognising themselves in a mirror and also being programmed with the human concepts of time and space.

It is essential that we refuse to have the connection between A.I. and the human race blurred and that this connection no longer remain unmonitored and unrestricted.

In 2016 a Hong Kong based company, Hanson Robotics activated a robot called Sophia. A Social Humanoid Robot, Sophia was granted citizenship in Saudi Arabia in 2017. This robot is very intricate and imitates human-like appearance and behaviour, copying human gestures and facial expressions.

As hybrid A.I. becomes a reality, humanity needs to tread with caution and secure very real boundaries. The great propagator of technological advancement, Elon Musk, has predicted that A.I. will overtake humans by 2025. Other experts in this field predict that by 2045 a 'human level machine intelligence' (HLMI) has a fifty percent change of occurring within the next 45 years.

The Max-Planck Institute has issued the results of a study that suggest humans would not be able to react fast enough, or smart enough, to prevent A.I. making its own decisions, over and above human control. Poorly regulated use of A.I. in weapons could have disastrous and catastrophic results.

Issues raised by the ideals of the founder and Executive Chairman of The World Economic Forum, Klaus Schwab, in his book "The Fourth Industrial Revolution" need to be given serious consideration. In fairness to the book, he lists positive and negative points to the new technologies driving this 'revolution'. The book also discusses the issues of new inter-connected A.I. and the impacts this emerging technology may have. It highlights the dangers of moving forward without an inclusive plan for humanity.

We are here at an auspicious time indeed. A time when we need to question the hidden motive behind any agenda for 'an inclusive plan for humanity.'

We are here, at an auspicious time indeed . A time when we need to be vocal in order to maintain our basic human rights and freedoms.

Question everything. Search for the truth and test it's frequency within your heart-based consciousness. For it is there that the real truth resides. Free from fear, free from control and prejudice.

An Auspicious Moment in Time

We are already witnessing mass implanting of microchips for cashless payment systems, and access to computers and buildings. Many employers are viewing this as an opportunity to implant micro chips into their workforce, to enhance their security systems.

Once implanted by their employer the microchipped worker might well ask; are they free individuals being paid for work, or the property of the company they work for?

A serious and seamless integration of human biology and technology is not in progress, as humans are being asked to volunteer to have a microchip implant in the brain that will connect them to a computer.

We are looking at Artificial Intelligence overriding our Subliminal Intuitive Intelligence.

Whilst some microchips are implanted in the hand, Elon Musk is initiating implants for use in the human brain. His company Neuralink has plans to put microchips in human brains by 2022.

The use of brain implants was initially only for neurological conditions like Alzheimers, yet we know it will fuse humankind with artificial intelligence. Neuralink has already broadcast a video of a monkey with a brain-chip playing computer games via chip-induced mind-control.

Whilst some may mistakenly look forward to playing computer games using this remote method, it has more sinister issues that demand controls be put in place. Computer hacking is a present day risk and reality. Imagine the disasters that could unfold if our brains are linked to an artificial intelligence which is then hacked?

The same Elon Musk owns SpaceX, a company that has already launched almost 2,000 Starlink satellites to date, with the intension of having some 40,000 in total. The purpose is to deliver high-speed broadband internet. They have already caused friction with Russia and China as they have almost caused collisions with their space stations and jeopardised anti-satellite missile tests.

Military issues aside, international astronomers have also filed complaints as the glare from the Starlink satellites already launched, has caused light pollution that obliterates the natural night sky.

Future generations may not be able to see the beauty of the natural star constellations as witnessed by humanity since creation. They will only see the bright geometric glare from the manmade net of 40,000 + Starlink satellites.

Does this seem like progress or the outrageous rape of our birthright and heritage? One man's ego and greed pitched against every humanitarian moral right?

Now, the same individual, claimed to be the richest man on earth, has purchased Twitter, one of the largest global social media platforms. Too much power?

We are here at an auspicious moment in time indeed. A time to be discerning in where we invest our time, our money, and our future.

We are a sentient species, that has gently evolved to be happy, social, emotional human beings. We laugh, we cry, we love. We have the ability to show incredible talents as we make music, art, food, love. We have the strength and ability to overcome great difficulties and challenges.

Humanity must awaken and embrace it's full potential. And we must do this in harmony with the synchronicity of Nature, not ego, not greed, not capital gain. We must continue to evolve, as all species have to date: through compassion and co-operation.

For it is **not** the survival of the fittest after all. It is **not** the one who has the biggest phallic rocket, who alone survives. It is certainly **not** the one who has the most money in the bank, who is the fittest.

It is through co-operation and compassion that humanity will progress, and survive. It is all about the survival of the species, and this will only originate through true humanitarian ethics.

Love and compassion will sustain our every need. It will calm every fear, and transcend every challenge.

The Microcosm and the Macrocosm

Our Earth is part of a whole Universe. The Universe is a part of a vast unexplored Multiverse. Were all living in 'The Mystery'.

This 'Mystery' is comprised of incredible, eternal, limitless energy. Always giving. Always nurturing. Always compassionate and overflowing with the essence of pure unconditional love.

Scientists would, very likely, label this energy as being an electro-magnetic substance. It is a frequency that can be measured and defined. We may all be familiar with the phrase 'as above - so below' and 'as within- so without'.

These sayings are pertinent.

Studies conclude that as the Earth has an electromagnetic energy field, so our bodies reflect the same structure.

Every single minute atom, is a mirror of the Universe itself. Inside every atom is a vast void, like outer space to our galaxy. The protons, neutrons and electrons inside every atom, are like our stars, planets and sun.

The Microcosm and the Macrocosm, the vast universe is reflected the smallest atom. Everything is energy and everything is connected and in a constant state of perpetual impermanence and change. A fascinating fluctuation of electromagnetic energies that continually resonate on various frequencies.

The Earth has a strong magnetic field, like an aura. The electromagnetic frequency inside this vortex is measured scientifically using the Schumann resonance. Earth's natural rhythm resonates from the frequency of 7.83Hz to 33.8Hz.

This frequency is the same frequency as an alpha/theta human brainwave that resonates when we are in a relaxed, dreamlike state. It is also the same frequency when healing and cell regeneration occurs in our body.

This frequency can be disturbed and distorted by modern technology like WiFi, cell phones, electrical appliances, the presence of nearby pylons etc.,.

This can cause an imbalance of our natural bodily bio-electromagnetic rhythm, causing dis-ease. The frequency of electromagnetic radiation that powers a cell phone, radio, or tv for example, ranges from 30,000Hz to 300billion Hz. A vast increase from our natural biorhythm of between 7.83Hz - 33.8Hz.

Scientific studies have concluded that:

> "exposure to strong electromagnetic fields in residential areas and in certain occupations, has been documented as significantly increasing the incidence or risk of cancer, heart disease, depression and other diseases. Certain groups of people such as the elderly, children, women who are pregnant and the weak have been found to be more sensitive or

susceptible to adverse effects from these fields..."

HeartMath Institute

It has been proven that when we are able to resonate in harmony with the planet's natural magnetic frequency we experience improved stress tolerance, calmness and an harmonious sense of well being.

When we are in harmony with Mother Earth's frequency, we resonate with health.

Our heart's magnetic field is our body's strongest rhythmic field. It resonates throughout every single cell of our body, and also extends out in all directions into the immediate environment around us. Using sensitive magnetometers, the heart's magnetic field can be effectively measured.

A group of Scientist in Northern California have been researching the science of the heart for over thirty years.

The HeartMath Institute

Known as the HeartMath Institute they have conducted an overwhelmingly large number of medical and scientific studies that advocate 'heart-coherence'. When our heart and mind work together in perfect harmony, in a 'heart-coherent' state, our heart frequency shifts to a resonance compatible with gratitude, happiness, co-operation and compassion.

HeartMath research has extended further afield to investigate the correlation between the magnetic fields of the Earth, and the magnetic field of the human heart. This project also researched into how this connection might improve the well-being of both Earth and Humanity.

By practicing heart-based meditations, it is possible to build a more heart-coherent world.

We are currently in the midst of intense global stress and strife. The old established order resonating through fear, anxiety, stress and control is on its last legs. The transition into the new era, the New Age of Aquarius will benefit greatly from people aligning with their deeper core heart energy. We will find that this is the frequency of the life-force going forwards.

Technology alone cannot solve all the problems we have. The problems that exist in the underlying foundations of current social constructs, and the catastrophic environmental problems that we perceive on a global scale, will not be solved by technology alone.

We have an infrastructure in place that can immediately alleviate much of the suffering experienced in the world today. For example, a small percentage, an estimated ten percent, of the world's current annual military expenditure, would feed, house and educate every person on Earth. Every person on Earth!

Why haven't we, as a species, taken the decision to implement these simple solutions?

What is it that is holding us back from making bolder, fairer, more compassionate decisions? Because the Collective Consciousness keeps us in a state of fear.

To activate the solution we require an essential global shift. A global shift in the Collective Consciousness.

As we collectively raise the electromagnetic frequency in our individual heart-based consciousness, so we lift the Collective Consciousness. Remember, it only takes the square root of 1% to effect the momentum required for such a collective awareness to become manifest.

The technology and infrastructure is already in place to allow us to experience a World based on co-operation and compassion. So, what is isolating us, holding us back from taking the plunge? It is the current state of our Collective Consciousness.

Since the late 1800s, scientist have been aware that the quality of the signals the heart sends to the brain profoundly affect our perceptions, brain functions and emotional experiences.

The heart sends more neurological signals to the brain than the brain sends to the heart.

The heart and brain communicate neurologically, energetically, and biochemically. The most important means of communication between the brain and the heart occurs neurologically via the transmission of nerve impulses.

Every time our heart beats, it creates a magnetic field that can be measured scientifically using a magnetometer. This magnetic field resonates within every cell in our body, and extends outside into our aura and beyond. The interaction of magnetic fields between individual people have been measured too.

Our brain and heart communicate biochemically through hormones and neurotransmitting chemicals. Our heart releases hormones, atrial peptides, and norepinephrine, and most importantly Oxytocin. It is a fact that the brain also releases Oxytocin as well as the heart.

When we experience heart-based consciousness, our brain and heart both release this 'happy hormone' creating a euphoric state of bliss.

The heart sends much more information to the brain than the brain sends to the heart. We may have been told as a child, 'think with your head not your heart,' or we may have heard the expression 'don't let your heart rule your head'. Yet this is indeed the very practice we need to implement.

Think with your heart - not your head! Let your heart rule your head!

The state of heart-coherence allows us to shift our inner perspective to one of appreciation, kindness, patience and compassion.

When we are in a state of heart-coherence our frequency is vibrant. When we are in a state of heart-coherence we find it impossible to be judgemental, angry, and stressed.

The heart is a source of emotional intelligence, and it transfers this intelligence to our emotions, strengthening our ability to effectively control them.

When we live our life in heart-coherence, studies have shown that we are likely to enjoy better health, better hormonal balance, improved immunity, lower blood pressure and a reduction in stress hormones.

Our heart is the source of emotional intelligence. Our heart can transfer intelligence to our emotions and strengthen our ability manage them, to process them.

Experiencing Heart-Based Consciousness

How do we open our heart energy?

How do we experience heart-based consciousness?

Firstly we need to begin to feel the energy that resides in our psyche. We must also remain calm and relaxed and not try too hard. When we come from a state of expectation, or when we are trying too hard to achieve, we are sabotaging ourselves from the outset.

We must first calm our mind, body and emotions. The easiest way to do this is to gently become aware of the breath.

Just notice how it enters your nostrils, don't alter the pace of breathing, just become aware of this most marvellous life-force energy.

The gentle rise and fall of our chest as we breathe is an ideal focus point to achieve calm, to feel appreciation for the miracle that we are.

How incredible that our breathing is so subtle, and yet so life-sustaining.

As we spend a few moments just gently breathing we can then calmly bring to mind a moment when our heart felt overwhelming compassion.

Maybe it was a beautiful sunset, or holding a new-born baby, or softly caressing a kitten or puppy. Just allow the frequency of compassion to enter your psyche and reside in your heart.

With every gently breath you breathe in, feel this resonance of compassion expanding as the petals of your heart chakra slowing open, sending the frequency of love throughout every atom of your being.

Staying calm and relaxed, and without trying, permit yourself to unwind into a delightful state of euphoria for as long as you can.
This is the blissful frequency of heart-based consciousness.

You might like to recite a few positive affirmations as you bring your session to a gentle close:

"I am at peace."

"I am a miracle, and I love who I am."

"Breathing in, I nurture myself. Breathing out, I nurture all creation."

As you gently return to normal consciousness, to the present moment, check in with your body and notice how expansive your heart energy feels. How much lighter and how much freer your entire energy system feels.

Humanity has been totally exhausted by decades of detachment from the truth. All truth.

The truth is, we are able to access our heart-based consciousness simply and easily. And by doing so on a regular basis we are also raising the collective consciousness.

Humanity, though totally exhausted by decades of detachment from the truth, is at last becoming empowered in a unified stance of non-compliance with the prevailing forces of fear and control.

Humanity is beginning to shift the collective consciousness, as it comes together in the frequency of unconditional love and compassion.

This seismic shift in the collective consciousness will assist humanity to become more enlightened.

A Blue-print for Mother Earth

Our incredible planet is a functioning part of the Galaxy, a part of the Universe, which in turn is part of a collective Multiverse.

Though small in the vast scheme of creation, our planet was designed with a purpose, a role to play. We humans were designed to be the custodians of this beautiful planet.

We were never designed to be enslaved to work, school, mortgage, rents, money, taxes, greed, fear and then death. Even death has been portrayed as oblivion, instilling more fear of the 'unknown'.

The truths is that we are eternal multidimensional beings. Powerful co-creators of our reality. Guardians of Mother Earth, and keepers of the Truth. We have been manipulated over eons to forget these truths. We have been played and enslaved.

The time for truth is now. This is an auspicious moment, we feel it, and we know it to be so.

Our energy is unique. The energy that forms Mother Earth is of unique importance not just to use, but to the entire Universe. The importance of what happens now will have repercussions throughout our Galaxy, and surrounding Galaxies, as yet unexplored by our scientific instruments.

Like the butterfly effect, every action produces a reaction. A tiny butterfly's wings might create tiny changes in the atmosphere that may one day ultimately alter the path of a tornado! Everything is connected.

Everything is energy and this energy is in a constant state of impermanence and change.

We have only to look around us to see evidence of historical and geographical change. Fossils show us that great creatures and incredible life forms lived before us.

We are constantly reminded that our climate is changing, and we are aware that there have been many Ice Ages in the past as our planet undergoes a rhythmic change.

However, the blueprint for Mother Earth has been defaced by the predominance of greed, with corporate ecocide on a devastating global scale.

Our Planet Earth has an electromagnetic field, similar to our own personal auric field. The Earth also has a rhythmic heart beat, just like our own.

We are intricately connected. The microcosm and the macrocosm. As within so without. As above so below. There is no separation.

When Mother Earth is abused we reap that devastation ourselves.

Mother Earth has been neglected, unloved, physically raped and despised and left for dead, by those guilty corporate ogres of greed, who would now seek another home on another planet.

As a species, we haven't been too clever. It would appear many of us have been in a day-dream. We have been sleepwalking our way to oblivion.

Humanity simply must re-connect with Mother Earth. We can swiftly relearn to adapt to her changing seasons, and to celebrate her ever-giving, ever-nurturing essence.

With careful control and with adequate restrictions in place, our technological achievements can ultimately work for us, rather than dominating and controlling us.

We already have the power, and the infrastructure to create paradise here on Earth.

The Power Is Within

Humans have evolved over time. Our brain is an intricate working mechanism that has evolved to protect us on a daily basis.

We can simplify the brain functions into three main parts.

NAME	LOCATION	PRIMARY FUNCTION
Brain 1: 'REPTILIAN BRAIN'	Amygdala & Cerebellum	Survival instinct Fight or Flight
Brain 2: 'MONKEY BRAIN'	Limbic System & Hippocampus	Stores Memories Relationships Connects Feelings & Controls Hormones
Brain 3: 'THINKING BRAIN'	Neocortex	Logic, Language, Forward Planning, Reasoning

Our 'Reptilian brain' has the basic functions under control, like breathing, alerting us when we are thirsty, or hungry. It also controls the flow of adrenaline, which in turn increases our heart rate, blood flow and alertness, originally giving us the ability to flee or fight.

In present day to day life, we often find we have far too much adrenaline in our system leading to anxiety and overwhelm. Adrenaline stays in our system for hours on end. When we first evolved we were designed to have an occasional threatening experience that might trigger and adrenaline rush.

Today we have too many adrenaline triggers. Our technology, especially our love affair with social media, ought to be held to account more, as it is triggering an almost continual state of anxiety, overwhelm and stress among many of us, especially the young and vulnerable.

Our 'Monkey Brain' is also being over-triggered by technology as it is responsible for our sociability. There is no question that our interaction with one another has been challenged and altered by social media. We have all heard people say "Lol" instead of actually laughing!

The delight once shared through smiling and laughing, giggling and expressing joy has now been reduced to a single syllable. Lol!

Our 'Thinking Brian' uses logic and analysis with rational thought. It is the seat of our morality as we analyse and control our emotional responses.

The electromagnetic energy that exists in our brain is often measured by scientists as they seek to explore and explain how we function. The scientific work that has been undertaken thus far, has proven that everything is connected, that everything is in a continual state of support and co-operation.

Later we look at the essential role of our unique individuality. We discuss the importance of retaining our Divine Sovereignty.

The Great Illusion

It is not about the survival of the fittest. That is an illusion.

It is about co-operation and compassion. It is about co-existing with the energy that is present. It is about evolving with the natural flow, not destroying nature and manufacturing implanted micro-chips!

Change has always historically come from grass-root movements. It evolves from the collective consciousness and morphs into reality. It has never successfully come from the top down. Only repression and oppression comes from the 'globalist elite' in a perceived downwards spiral. In truth we, the honest majority, are far higher placed in morality and spirituality than they!

In the following chapters we examine simple tweaks to the existing infrastructure that can bring about a utopian lifestyle with minimum effort, and maximum benefit.

We will endure and survive radical change. The current system will very likely have to break entirely, with possible ensuing chaos, before we can enjoy the radical rebuilding, which will be done in the spirit of compassion and cooperation for all life on earth.

Question Everything

It can not be stated enough times: question everything.

Find the answers in publications and bonafide websites that have accountability. We simply need to use our rational thought to process and discern what is genuine. Living as we are, in the era of misinformation, manipulation, disinformation, and deception.

Take information into your heart and assess it there too. If it resonates comfortably it is likely to be true. If it feels false, fearful and frightening, then question it and discard it.

As we look within to question our motivation, we may be very surprised at what we find.

Often we discover that our thoughts and ideas are not actually ours! They have been accumulated over many years and many scenarios and from many sources.

As we have already discussed, The Collective Consciousness, as it's name suggests, this is the accumulation of all human awareness or thought. On a parr with and often linked to the Akashic records, this phenomenon has a powerful influence on our day to day habitual thought.

Just as ants and bees are able to learn new habits across continents from one ant or bee braking new thought patterns - so we realise that, we too, can be at the cutting edge of raising or lowering humanity as a whole.

Individually, each of us is a miraculous, creative energy force, blessed by Creator with the virtues of Trust and Free Will.

We have the free will to destroy and deplete, or to cure and enhance.

At every opportunity we can either act to benefit the highest and greatest good of all, or not.

The still, small voice within, encourages us to act in harmony with the Divine. We all hear it or sense it. We all know what the right thing to do is.

The gift of Free Will, bestowed upon each one of us by the Divine Creator, allows us to decide which path to take. And we are also made aware that our choice will have consequences and repercussions be they good or bad or indifferent.

Even when we make irrational or detrimental decisions, or when we choose not to act against injustice, our heart-based consciousness prompts us to acknowledge truth.

We can carry blame as a burden and grudges as toxic blockages for many years, perhaps even an entire lifetime.

By holding on to the past misdeeds and negative emotions we are effectively imprisoning ourselves. Building a prison - a gilded cage where our sacred energy becomes stagnant and we become more detached from our true harmonious self: our Higher Self.

We are hard-wired for health, and happiness. It is an unnatural effort to resonate on the lower coarse vibrations of guilt, blame, anger, fear. They are not conducive to wellness.

Our Subconscious mind records everything. It is always alert and awake. It is generally accepted that our subconscious mind is like an incredibly efficient computer hard-drive that comprises around 95per cent of our thought process.

It loves repetition and habits, and although it has no verbal language, it can communicate or 'speak' to us through images, when we dream. Our subconscious mind takes onboard everything literally and makes no judgement or logical analysis.

Although Humanity may be totally exhausted by decades of detachment from the truth, it is ready to open to a great transformational shift of consciousness.

Scientists, and philosophers alike are aware that new Galactic frequencies are entering our solar system, creating a shift in our mental awareness. We are witnessing a shift on a Subconscious level and a profound, transformational energy shift in enlightenment on the Collective Consciousness level.

In days gone by a Guru may have fasted and meditated in a cave for a period of anything up to a month, with the aim of achieving a higher degree of enlightenment. We are now aware that we are able to tap into that energy the Guru created, and achieve enlightenment in a much shorter duration, whilst also living and working under a restricting third-dimensional framework.

And so it is, that now, at this profound significant moment, that many of us feel called to raise our collective energy in order to assist others in achieving enlightenment, through transforming the energy of the Collective Consciousness.

The Significance of the Present Moment

We have all very likely noticed that things are not how they used to be!

It may be quite frustrating to see old solid institutions crumbling, like our much treasured National Health Service, our transport and infrastructures ,the education system, the financial sector and the very systems of government we have become so used to.

The 'old ways' all appear to be breaking apart.

They are breaking apart.

They are breaking apart because they are in the transformational process of realigning with the new incoming frequencies of The New Age of Aquarius, also referred to as the new fifth dimension.

Some of the existing infrastructures will survive and provide the groundwork for the new systems.

Examples of some out of dated systems are:
top-down government
stock exchanges
GDP for measuring progress
fossil fuels
animal agriculture
private ownership
excessive/obscene wealth

slave labour
cruelty of any kind
war/ violence
crime
celebrity status

Examples of the new future systems are:
new penal systems - involving meditation and yoga
not for profit corporate projects
new methods of learning and healing
lighter bodies - less food required
more leisure time for joyful pursuits
revival of the arts,
new sports activities
no comparison/competition
Respect. Honour. Dignity. Compassion.

Our Ego has in the past sought to make others wrong, in order for 'it' to be right!

Individual ego has been complicit in the 'Divide and Conquer' programme. Competing to be the best, have the biggest, be the strongest, own the most etc.,.

As we transform in harmonious alignment with the new incoming energies, our ego will adapt too, and will begin to naturally resonate with the frequencies of cooperation and compassion. All life on Earth will be lifted and affected in a positive way from these new energy patterns.

Many of us today are here to bring these higher frequencies to Earth.

Many of us have an inner knowing that we were always destined for a specific purpose at this particular time and in this particular lifetime.

Some of us are labelled, or identify ourselves as, Indigoes, Star Seeds, Rainbows, Pleiadians, Arcturians, and many more! In the next few chapters we will look at these individual groups and the importance of us collectively anchoring the light into the World and how this can be done.

Part Two

Past Deceptions and Hidden Truth

The Realm of Limitation

The Great Connection

Leylines

Ancient Civilisations

Old Science - New Revelations

Sunken Cities & The Bermuda Triangle

How and Why Earth Shifts Occur

Standing Stones & Astronomy

Inter-Galactic Intervention

The Realm of Limitation

As a species, we are not very smart are we?

We often view the animal kingdom with an air of arrogance and superiority, yet should we be so smug? After all, animals don't have mortgages, they are not enslaved to a monetary system that requires them to sacrifice their life to work and an endless stream of debt and anxiety! They do not plunder the planet's resources! They do not take more than they need!

We have been duped! Deceived! Tricked!

We spend our lives in a constant state of stress, in an ambitious cycle of acquisition, social status, ownership, material gain, debt, and then - death.

Of all the many things we learn in life, we are never taught what to expect at the point of death, though death is the one and only sure thing that we are all going to experience. No one escapes death!

One of the biggest deceptions ever pulled on humanity was the concept of Hell.

This somewhat fantastical religious concept placed a powerful and extremely fearful energy into what would otherwise be a natural sequence of events.

Just as we cannot recall our own birth, (though our mother's doubtless do!) we were part of the process, we emerged and we were born into the Physical Plane.

The Physical Plane, a realm of limitation. We signed up for this life of limitation, which though limited in every sense, is none the less amazing in its variety and abundant sensory experiences.

Our physical life is limited. Limited in so far as it will definitely expire at some point. Our body will cease to function for one reason or another and we will find our selves at the point of death, or transition, a preferable, less formidable, expression.

Our sensory perceptions are limited during our lifetime, as we cannot perceive Ultra Violet Light, or Infra Red Light. Science teaches us that these frequencies exist but we cannot perceive the full spectrum. We only see approximately 1% of the light spectrum. There is a whole other 99% is going on beyond our perception.

Similarly we cannot hear all the sound frequencies that exist. Dog whistles, radio waves and other sound phenomena are beyond our limited physical perception.

Yet this life of limitation, with all its restrictions, is one that we have all signed up for. For now at least.

We know that like attracts like, and as we 'die', so our physical body returns to the physical realm, it basically begins to decompose almost immediately. Our spiritual energy is likewise drawn back to the spiritual realm at the point of death/ transition . We are naturally drawn to that loving light-frequency that is our true home.

This is realm that we often hunger for when we are separated from it by physical distractions and experiences.

Many people go through life with a fear of death and dying. This fear is often such a strong overwhelming resonance that it undermines the function of the physical, emotional and mental aspects of an individual. We know that like attracts like, and that fear creates dis-ease, which magnifies and manifests as physical disease.

There is a great deal of evidence that proves that we are not temporary beings, but that we are eternal spiritual energies. There is no death, there is only transition. Energy cannot be destroyed, it an only be transformed. And we are bundles of electro-magnetic energy!

There is so much evidence of reincarnation and our gift of freewill and life everlasting.

I run many workshops and one to one session on past life recall, and have written extensively on the subject in other books.

I recommend researching the work of Professor Ian Stevenson who scientifically analysed hundreds of cases, proving the case for reincarnation.

Why would we be duped, lied to and tricked into believing and fearing that this is our one and only chance at life, and that from here it is either heaven or hell for all eternity?

We can clearly see and sense that the benefits go to those who wish to keep us in a state of confusion, and fear.

Let go of the fear of dying, for there is no death. Just a glorious renewal and continuation.

We are part of a wonderful cosmic energy that loves us and nurtures us and most likely, at this particular epic moment in time, even feels pity for us!

It is time to take back control over our destiny. As an intelligent species are we not entitled to know the truth about our essence, about the extent of our true potential?

The Great Connection

GeoBiology is a relatively new science that studies the interconnectedness of Earth's biosphere and eco systems, and the material makeup of the physical planet itself.

We are aware that everything is connected, and everything is energy. Everything is in a constant flux of impermanence and change.

Guiding that change on this amazing planet, are energy patterns known as Ley Lines.

These ancient energy tracts were respected by our ancestors who often understood them to be places of extraordinary power, especially the nodes, where two lines intersect or cross each other.

Glastonbury for example is a well established powerful energy centre where major ley lines of Mary and Michael intersect.

There is phenomenal research being undertaken by well accredited individuals like Rory Duff. I recommend all his work for further research.

He has revealed through his research and dowsing training, that the Ley Lines vary in size and width and resonance. He has monitored various ley lines in different continents, and has revealed that they come together in harmonious alignment during the Equinoxes and Solstices.

He has also established that the duration of the harmonious resonance on the ley lines has, over the recent past years, increased.

The energy of the four equinoxes has extended from one or two days to last over 20 days.

At the present rate of ley-line energy expansion Rory Duff indicates that by 2024 we will have 365 day solstice resonance. It will be like Christmas every day!

Leylines

It is possible that in ancient times humanity cultivated a greater understanding of the link between science, nature, geometry, mathematics and astronomy. It is possible that ancient civilisations lived a more harmoniously attuned life than we currently experience.

The Australian aborigines follow the 'Dreaming Track' as they go 'walk-about' through the harsh and rugged natural terrain of Australia. An environment consider hostile to modern, 'civilised' man, the aborigines 'see' energy lines.

Similarly the Chinese philosophy of Feng Sui senses and honours the ancient energy lines. The art and science of Feng Sui respects and enhances the Dragon lines.

It is often believed that Other-worldly beings instructed our ancestors of the significance of the sacred energy places. Speculation abounds as to where ancient civilisations acquired their knowledge.

It has been scientifically proven that the position where Leylines cross, or intersect (known as a node) stronger frequencies of geomagnetic resonance can be tangibly measured. There are different types of nodes and more technical analysis can be found by studying the research of Rory Duff. His work is ongoing and attracting more interest as global awareness increases.

It is unsurprising that many of our great spiritual sites, churches, stone circles, and monuments were built on these nodes.

Geo-biologists are aware that the recent surge in human celebration and activity at sacred sights like Stonehenge and other known ley-line nodes, has assisted the light frequency to become more activated. Group activity ignites the Collective Consciousness and this has a profound effect on the energetic frequencies being sent to Mother Earth.

These frequencies are received by Mother Earth, and are relayed back into our physical space via the ley lines. Such a magnificent interplay of giving and receiving. An interplay which has been forgotten over recent times, and needs to be mindfully reinstated.

As the resurgence in reviving ancient pagan celebrations and rituals, at these energy sites has grown, so too has the energy on these nodes flourished, and the Leylines have become more vibrant in frequency.

Another contributing factor comes from outside our galaxy.

According to NASA the large inter-galactic gamma-rays are impacting on Earth with an increasing frequency. Gamma-rays are the most intense blasts of light.

They are considered by astronomers to be the most powerful energy in the Universe.

An interplay of energy on a much grander scale. Microcosm and macrocosm.

Everything is connected.

Everything is energy, and its all interwoven one within the other.

Even what we consider to be 'empty space' is not a void at all. It too is energy. It carries sound waves and light frequencies, and has potent electro magnetic energy surging through it.

Everything is energy and energy is light. Even perceived darkness isn't devoid of light. Darkness is energy with less light.

Only light can dispel darkness, transforming it into lighter energy.

Later we look at how this phenomenon can be used during our ascension process.

Ancient Civilisations

The Mayan Calendar plays significant role in our great awakening. It drew the attention of the world to the great planetary alignment of 2012.

We are now aware that this was far from the cataclysmic end of the world as interpreted by main stream media! Far from it! It was the birth of new Great Age. The Golden Age of Aquarius. Yet bizarrely the Mayan Calendar also calculated the planetary movements hundreds of years before the actual Mayan civilisation, and also hundreds of years after it ceased to exist.

What did exist pre-Mayan culture? How far back in time can we go? Modern History teaches us that civilisation and modern man is 5k years old.

The following chart gives us a fascinating insight into the various ancient civilisations and their timeline.

Two of these ancient cultures still exist today and carry a wealth of wisdom that will benefit humanity as we transition into the future frequencies.

The Dogan have a vast and complex understanding of the Universe and the movement and of the star constellations. This ancient culture holds the traditional belief that they originated from the star constellation of Sirius.

They were able to predict the trajectory of the star Sirius 'B' which was unknown to western astronomers, and invisible to the naked eye. The star Sirius 'B' was only discovered in 1862, long after the Dogan had told their tale to the western world.

And there are far more curious, and challenging tales to be told from other ancient civilisations.

Their traditions, and their technological abilities, indicate that mankind has reached intellectual levels of intelligence in the past.

ANCIENT CIVILISATIONS:

AZTEC	1325 - 1521 AD	MEXICO
INCAS	1438 - 132 AD	PERU
MAYAN	2600 - 900 AD	MEXICO, HONDURAS & EL SALVADOR
PERSIA	550 - 331 BC	EGYPT, TURKEY
CHINESE	1600 - 1046 BC	CHINA
INDUS	2600 - 1900 BC	INDIA, PAKISTAN
GREECE	2700 - 479 BC	ITALY, N.AFRICA, FRANCE
PERU	3000 - 1800 BC	PERU
EGYPT	3150 - 30 BC	NILE
DANUBE	5500 - 3500 BC	DANUBE, BALKANS
MESOPOTAMIA	6500 - 539 BC	IRAQ, TURKEY, SYRIA

CHINA/JIAHU	7000 - 5700 BC	HENAN CHINA
AIN GHAZAL	7299 - 5000 BC	JORDAN
CATAL HOYUK	7500 - 5700 BC	TURKEY
AUSTRALIA	5000 - PRESENT DAY	AUSTRALIA
DOGAN	3200 - PRESENT DAY	MALI

There are many phenomenal sites around the world that hold incredible secret information.

Most of us are familiar with Stonehenge and the Pyramids as being wonders of the world. There are others too. Some are just coming to light and excavations are ongoing.

1. GOBEKLI TEPE / MODERN SYRIA & TURKEY

It is older than Stonehenge and older than Great Pyramids in Egypt. In fact it is estimated to be 12,000 years old, and 8,000 years before the bible predicted creation! It has taken 13yrs to discover just 5% of it site.

This ancient site was only uncovered in 1994. When it was discovered it changed everything that was previously known about history of mankind.

Gobekli Tepe is a massive, ancient temple but out of pillars organised into great stone rings. There are more than 200 pillars in 20 circles that were discovered through geophysical surveys.

Each pillar has a phenomenal height of 20ft. and weighs up to 10 tons. They are fitted into sockets that were hewn out of the local rock. The exact details of the site's function remain a mystery.

This was clearly an advanced society as these circular temples contained hieroglyphs and detailed astronomical knowledge. These building also appear to have been mysteriously deliberately buried.

Like so many massive stone structures, we simply do not know why it was built, how it was built and what is what used for.

Gobekli Tepe is significant as it profoundly changes the understanding of the development of human society, overturning precious assumptions. The capabilities of this culture were beyond our expectations for that period of time.

2. GULF OF CAMBAY / GULF OF KAMBHAT INDIA

One of the oldest sunken cities lost for thousands of years under 120ft of water it is believed to have been sunken underwater when ice caps melted at the end of the last ice age some 9k years ago.

The flood has been mentioned in many religious writings including the Bible.

Hundreds of artefacts were collected and scientific studies were undertaken to prove that the artefacts were genuine.

3. OLMEC CULTURE

The Olmec were the predecessors of pre-hispanic Mexico.

Their civilisation was in existence 1500-1200 BC and emerged independently like India, Egypt, China, Sumaria, and Peru.

The Olmec are known for their famous colossal stone head statues. Yet their culture contributed much to modern humanity:

competitive sports - cyclical calendars - complex government - maths - astronomy - agriculture (they cultivated tomatoes, beans, sweet potatoes, squash, manioc, and maize.)

The Olmec also had a complex alphabet and their writing is very similar to early Chinese.

Why does the existence of these ancient civilisations not tally with what we are taught?

What else has been hidden or not acknowledged?

Old Science - New Revelations

Let's look at some artefacts that are out of place if we believe the old science that stated civilisation and modern man is 5k years old.

According to old science of evolution, of Darwin's theory, there were only amoeba around when these artefacts existed:

1. a clay human figure found in Idaho dated 1.2million years old

2. a micro chip in a Russian rock dated 250million years old

3. a human foot print in New Mexico dated 290million years ago

4. a hammer in Texas dated 400 million years old

5. 'non-earth' alloy spheres in South Africa dated 570million years old.

Quite a lot of what we thought, or rather what we were taught, is being revealed as a deception. The hidden truth is coming to light. Question everything!

Darwin's publication of "The Origin of Species" purported the theory based on survival of the fittest. The philosophy that life evolves according to the most survival of the fittest contains a flaw which Darwin himself was aware of: if man evolved from apes, where is the 'missing link' the part-ape part-man prototype?

Life survives through adaptation and cooperation. It's not the survival of the fittest, but the survival of the inspirational innovator!

Homo sapiens came into existence some 750,000 years ago. Scholars and Archeologists both agree that somewhere around 3,000BC mankind took a mega leap forward.

This quantum leap forward was with regards to technology and civilisation. Scholars and Archeologists can only speculate as to what provoked this shift towards a new advanced human culture of excelling in communication, art, agriculture and community.

So much of the past is speculation and wonder! We marvel at the existence of large standing stones and megaliths all over the globe. The Pyramids, and phenomenal stone structures never cease to fascinate us, with so many suggestions and theories as to their purpose and origin.

Many legends suggest that visitors from outer space came to build these incredible monuments.

In Carnac in North West France there is a stretch of over 3,000 megalithic stones stretching over two miles long. To date, it is the largest collection of such standing stones on Earth. It has been dated between 4,500 - 2,500 BC. The intersecting lines, circles and triangles form intricate geometric patterns, yet they predate the concept of geometry by two thousand years!

These standing stones are highly visible from the sky. They can be seen quite clearly from space, and local legends say that giants built them!

In common with other standing stones, like Avebury and Stonehenge, the stones at Carnac have strong, electro-magnet frequencies around them.

Are the answers lost in history? Can we only speculate as to what really has occurred on this spectacular planet?

There is much evidence to support the theory of inter-planetary assistance with human evolution on earth. This evidence supporting the existence of extraterrestrial intervention is right here, in plain sight. As we research different cultural legends, and various global ancient religions, we can see that 'people from the sky' are a common phenomenon.

Zeus, Thor and Sirius were all Gods that came from the sky, from the stars. Is this just pseudo-science, or is there some truth in the theory that we are not alone in this vast Universe.

The Sun may account for 99.86% of our Solar mass, but it is only a mere 0.000000000000000000000000000000001% of the Universe. And we may be existing in a Multi-verse not a Uni-verse, there may be far more to Creation that we can even begin to imagine!

Whether it is pseudo-history, or fact, we are wise to keep an open mind and respect the research carried out by authors like Immanuel Velikovsky, Sitchin, and Erich von Daniken.

The latter, suggests that the Anunnaki, mentioned in Sumerian myths were also 'Gods from the Sky', in other words ET's. In his book "Odyssey of the Gods' he suggests that the Anunnaki were searching for minerals, especially gold which they found and mined on the African continent.

Sitchin's research ties in with Biblical texts. He released his book "The Twelfth Planet", in 1976 (followed by a further seven books) and became the most prolific and important proponent of ancient astronaut hypothesis.

Zachariah Sitchin was born in 1920 in Azerbaijan and lived in Palestine. He attributed the creation of ancient Sumerian culture to the Anunnaki, who he suggested were a race of extra-terrestrials from the planet Niburu, beyond Neptune. He claimed that Sumerian mythology suggested that this planet has a 3,600 year long elliptical orbit around the Sun.

We may well question everything. Why are there so many standing stones, and huge ancient monuments, that are so visible from outer space? Why do they exist all over the globe, even under our oceans? Why are there mysterious legends of Atlantis, Lemuria, and other long gone civilisations? And as we ponder and marvel at these questions, the hypothesis that visitors from other Galaxies came here to Earth seems highly likely.

Plato wrote two books around 360BC about advanced civilisations that existed 9,000 years before his time! Ancient greek texts suggest that Atlantis had Extra Terrestrial connections and was founded by Poseidon.

Whatever these ancient texts reveal, be it fact or fiction, we are being presented today with evidence of some very mysterious, and curious findings. For example, the DNA from an 8,000 year old fossilised skeleton, found in a cave in Paclicci, Italy, has revealed a human with a larger brain. Evidence that is thought provoking, insofar as it contradicts what we were taught about the past.

What other hidden truths and past deceptions will be uncovered in the near future.

Did Aliens intervene to speed up the advancement of humans, as they took that giant leap forward in sometime around 3,000 BC?

Is it a co-incidence that this is the exact same period that the pyramids were built?

Were the legendary gods described in ancient myths really aliens?

Have they intervened before and are they intervening now?

We could spend a lifetime delving into these curious questions!

Keep an open mind and question everything. And as we do so, more historical facts are revealed, challenging what we have been taught, and opening more fascinating portals for us to explore. As we do so, we are better equipped to deal with our current situation.

Sunken Cities and The Bermuda Triangle

We remain entranced by the legends of Atlantis and Lemuria. Ancient civilisations that were 'under the sea'. Scientists are finding out that these legends may not be completely fictitious.

We often refer to Earth as 'The Blue Planet', as Oceans and Seas cover over 71% of our Earth. As marine archeologists explore this vast unknown they are discovering very sophisticated relics on the sea bed that are over 10,000 years old.

This questions the theory of evolution, and suggests that we are older than we thought!

Everything is in a state of importance and change. The World has not always appeared as we know it now. And it will keep changing.

During the last ice age, ocean levels were lower as Europe was covered in a shield of ice over 2 miles high. Some 21,000 years ago as the ice began melting, approximately 10 millions square miles of land was flooded. To give us some idea of the scale of the flood, we can imagine it as the same size as the land masses of Europe and China combined.

Researchers suggest that there are believed to be in excess of 200 sunken townships and cities in the Mediterranean Sea alone!

Just off the coast of the Bahamas a complex ancient city harbour has been discovered and off the Coast of Cuba, stone structures with wide avenues have been found, which were submerged around some 6,000 yeas ago. Astonishingly some of these structures include pyramids.

The legend of Atlantis has often been associated with the Bahamas, Cuba and the Bermuda Triangle.

This large region of the North Atlantic Ocean includes the southeastern coast of the USA, Bermuda, Cuba, Hispaniola, Jamaica, the Greater Antilles, and Puerto Rico.

A very strange vortex of energy is understood to exist in this expansive area, where many unexplained occurrences have occurred. Military aircraft have disappeared with no wreckage ever found. Electrical equipment, navigational aids, seem to have difficulty operating efficiently in this peculiar area.

Centuries ago the voyager, Christopher Columbus, reported seeing peculiar, large, disc-like vehicles rising into and out of the Ocean in this area, off the boast of Bermuda.

There is a little known area just south of Japan, Yonaguni Island, where the energy is just as mysterious as the Bermuda Triangle. The similarities are phenomenal. Planes and ships disappear, radar and radio links vanish and no mobile network exists in this area. Japan has declared this as a 'disaster zone'.

In 1987 a massive sunken city was discovered in this 'disaster zone', including a large pyramid structure.

Nicknamed Japan's Atlantis, this phenomenal underwater site is believed to be more that 6,000 years old.

The five-layered pyramid is the size of two football fields, and has large megaliths with human faces carved on them. Ancient Japanese legends suggest objects rise up and out of the sea and flying the air in this area, similar to the reports around the Bermuda Triangle.

Both Yonaguni Island, Japan, and the Bermuda Triangle are on the 25degree North longitude. Both have the same mysterious magnetic energy which causes physical objects to vanish without trace. Is this merely a coincidence, or evidence of phenomenal portals of metaphysical energy.

We are re-learning and re-writing history as hidden truths come to light at last.

At a time when mainstream archeology tells us there were not cities, that we were living in caves, we now have evidence that proves there were cities dating back some thirty-one thousand years and more!

In Armenia there is a henge of circular stones that is four thousand years older that Stonehenge.

Hindu scholars have also stated that their culture goes back in time beyond conventional teachings in the West. The latest discovery 200 miles north of the city of Khambhat, (also known as Cambay), of a submerged city known as Dwarka.

This ancient legendary city of Dwarka has cobbled streets and temples.

Mythology records that this city was destroyed by what we can now recognise and liken to a nuclear bomb. This is not just a myth but a hidden truth.

How and Why Earth Shifts Occur

The Earth wobbles on its axis and constellations therefore move in and out of view. Our Earth shifts approximately every 2,600 years or so. Sometimes this shift and wobble is slow and gradual, and sometimes it is dramatic and fast.

A shift in the Earth's axis causes major climate changes, including flooding and loss of life. We can deduce from the evidence above that great civilisations have existed here on Earth and have ceased to thrive due to unforeseen, or uncontrollable circumstances.

Some former civilisations may have been many times more intelligent that we are today. We can only speculate on the evidence presented. It seems plausible that at some point earlier civilisations may have attained a similar level of technological intelligence and expertise that we have today. It seems highly likely that atomic warfare may have caused annihilation at a previous point in time. It is there in the Hindu records.

Everything is energy and this energy is in a constant state of impermanence and change. Nothing is static, not even a mountain as small stones and grains of sand move constantly. The inner earth erupts at will causes impermanence and change too.

Our magnetic North and South poles are in transition and scientists agree that the time has come for them to reverse. The last time this polar reversal occurred was some 780,000 years ago. We are able to tell this by studying volcanic rock formations and how the iron deposits changed direction during this time.

At the present moment it is believed that the north pole has moved at an accelerated rate from 6 miles to 32 miles per year. The energy from the magnetic poles creates the magnetic field around our Earth, rather like an aura, that protects us from solar radiation and other frequencies.

Our Sun has magnetic poles too, and these reverse every 11 years. We are currently in Solar Cycle 25

All the signs indicate that we are currently at a cusp, at the very edge of great change. Many of us have a deep inner knowing that we were called to Earth at this particular time to assist in the shift, in the Earth and in Humanity and all life on Earth.

We are multidimensional beings, experiencing a short sensory experience here on Earth. We are co-creators of our reality, Gods and Goddesses, Guardians of Mother Earth.

We appear to be like a small speck of dust in the grand scheme of things. If our Galaxy, the Milky Way, were scaled down to the size of Europe, Earth would be a saucer somewhere France - and we would be a minuscule microbe on that saucer!

Looking within, we know we are more than a microbe on a saucer, more than a mere spec of dust!

So much more!

Standing Stones & Astronomy

As we have just exited a 5,125 yearly cycle of confusion and conflict, can we now embrace a new 5,125 yearly cycle of peace and co-operation?

This Great Cycle of Time is by no means the largest period of time to be astrologically measured.

It is, in fact, only one fifth of the Great Platonic Year which is the total period it takes for all the planets and fixed stars complete a total return. This amazing Great Platonic Year measures some 26,000 years!

These Great Ages of time are not part of astronomy, they are astrological ages, based on the twelve constellations of the Zodiac. Their trajectory is retrograde hence the Age preceding the Age of Aquarius, was the Age of Pisces and before that the Age of Aries, which is defined by the years 2200BC - 100BC.

There are massive great standing stones around the globe. Every continent hosts some gigantic monument of some kind. These, as we have discussed already, can be seen primarily from outer space. They also have accurate alignment to Star Constellations.

How did 'primitive' mankind erect such huge stone monuments? What purpose lay behind such technical and laborious work?

There are so many curious questions that arise when we explore this peculiar phenomenon. Like the proverbial elephant in the room, they stand there, testimony of a former intelligence.

Many of these global stone structures weigh over 15tonnes and can be seen from outer space, like beacons or markers. In Carnac, France there are some 3,000 massive stones forming intricate geometric shapes, squares, and circles. Within this area there is a strong geomagnetic force field.

It is truly fascinating to research the science behind acoustic levitation and the anti-gravity.

Scientific research is currently shedding light on sonar sound waves that may have been used by ancient civilisations to create an anti-gravitational vortex to move the 20 ton rocks that were used in some of the ancient stone monuments.

Inter-Galactic Intervention

One of the biggest hidden truths may be that of inter-galactic intervention.

The world famous actress Shirley MacLaine risked her entire career when she published "Out on a Limb" in the 1980's. An autobiographical book it details amongst other events, her trip to Peru and her contact with an individual from the star constellation Pleiades.

In her book she evidences that many USA Presidents have been aware of the intervention on Earth with Pleiadian beings. Kennedy, Reagan and Carter all knew about these star beings who amongst other ideals, wanted to share their knowledge of free energy.

Could that be the reason their interaction with us has been kept hidden. Fossil fuel companies would certainly not be amused!

Around the same time "Light Years" was written and published by Billy Meier which contained photographic evidence of Pleiadian Light Ships. He writes that the Pleiadians and their Council of Nine are here to assist with getting Gaia, Mother Earth, back on track with her original divine blueprint.

Most of the contents of this particular book have, in fact, been channelled through me, by the wisdom of the Pleiadian Council of Nine since 2020. Many may find the notion of Inter-Galactic Intelligence unfamiliar and uncomfortable.

In the preceding pages of this book we have seen the use of scientific, and factual evidence that proves many other civilisations have come and gone on this Earth.

We have also witnessed that the presence of 'other worldly' intelligence was evidenced throughout those civilisations, and that it is being hidden in plain sight from us today.

Channelling from the higher realms of reality is something we look at in the next chapter as we explore techniques to elevate our own personal energy frequency to access these higher, intelligent frequencies for ourselves.

**Indigo, Crystal and Starseeds,
Arcturians, and Andromedans,
Sirians, and Pleiadians**

There are many here on Earth at this auspicious moment in time, who have chosen to incarnate to assist in the evolutionary process of ascension. Many of these individuals would associate with the one or other of the above categories.

Many of us have a profound memory of coming here for a specific purpose, and some of us have temporarily become absorbed in the physical attractions of the third dimension and have forgotten what that purpose was!

One of the main purposes of this book is to assist in awakening that memory, to offer simple explanations and techniques that will rekindle ancient awareness and spiritual connections beyond this space and time.

Many old souls, and groups of galactic volunteers, have chosen to incarnate here during this auspicious time. Many of these souls have been aware of their calling for a long time. They are here to assist with the great shift into the 5th dimensional consciousness.

Often these souls have very difficult paths in life here. Many of these masterful souls are here to raise the frequencies from the worst, lowest vibrations. Many are also specialists in fields like teaching, healing, and have an intuitive knowledge beyond their apparent years.

These souls are advanced and carry galactic coding within their DNA, they hold the template for the New Earth. They specialise in fields that open new ways of living, as we develop the new paradigm.

These advanced souls have come here, at this time from higher realms, from distant planets, and from other solar systems and galaxies.

The Earth is important in the grander scheme of things. This urgent energy shift, this necessary ascension from the depths of destruction, and despair will simply not be allowed to fail.

The Pleiadians are particularly concerned with the development of our planet Earth. The Pleiadian Council of Nine are assisting Gaia back to her Original Divine Blue Print.

Everything is connected and it is central to the Universe that Earth doesn't fail this momentous challenge this time.

The Pleiades are a group of seven sister stars, in the constellation of Taurus, with Alcyone being the largest star, and known as the "Central One". They are approximately some 400 light years from Earth, around 2,351 trillion miles away, yet the telepathic and spiritual connection is undeniably strong.

Billy Meier, in his book "Light Years" had direct contact with actual Pleiadian beings, as did Shirley McClaine. It is also purported that World Leaders Kennedy, Regan and Jimmy Carter were also in contact with beings from this dimension.

The Pleiadian teachings are of world peace, and bringing knowledge of alternative energy systems that would not harm Earth.

If we are in any doubt about Inter-Galactic communication, let us remember that the Hubble Telescope discovered around 10,000 new galaxies in just 10 days!

Pleiadians wish to assist us here on Earth because they had apparently experienced a war that destroyed their original home planet in the Lyra Constellation.

They have communicated that Earth has been destroyed twice before by its own inhabitants and they wish to help prevent this happening again.

The wisdom from higher inter-galactic realms is currently pouring down onto Mother Earth and is being channelled globally by many individuals.

As we begin to stand in our own truth, and accept the knowledge that is resonating within, so our psyche begins to transform.

Our basic lower energies begin to ascend as we become more enlightened.

Historically, other civilisations have also been aware of the Pleiadians:

1. The Incas of Peru speak of them.

2. The Chinese Civilisation in 2357 BC mention them too.

3. The Greeks aligned temples to the rising of Alcyone.

4. In Egypt the Great Pyramid is aligned so that on the first day of Spring the South Passageway frames Pleiades.

5. The Samoans of the South Pacific call their sacred bird "The Bird of the Pleiades."

6. In Japan on Mayday, the Feast of the Lanterns stems from an ancient rite to honour the Pleiades.

7. The Hopi call Pleiades Choo-ho-kan which means "Home of Our Ancestors."

8. The legends of the Navajo tell how mankind originated from Pleiades, and that we continue to be visited by them.

There can be very little argument against the presence of inter-galactic intelligence. Only a very closed mind, a very egocentric 3rd dimensionally bound person, would find the evidence produced thus far questionable.

The current news media have coined the phrase "conspiracy theory" which implies the believer of such a theory is a total crank, not to be trusted or believed.

How can theories possibly be categorised as conspiratorial!?

The current news media outlets held to account by those deluded parasites who have accumulated vast obscene amounts of wealth, wish to limit any form of free thinking.

To them, the threat of free thinking them, is the biggest threat of all.

Compliance and control, are the bywords of the global so called 'elite'.

Is his why there is so much fluoride in the tap water we are encouraged to drink?

While the masses are doped up in a haze of fluoride-induced stupor, sleep-walking through a monotonous life, atrocities are taking place before our very eyes. Whilst our senses are numbed and dumbed by being plugged into the internet at every available opportunity, crimes against humanity go unheeded, and ecocide devastates the very environment we need to survive! Madness reigns!

The Pleiadians and other inter-galactic beings must be watching this scenario and scratching their heads in astonishment at what we have done and what we are complicit in allowing to be done.

The saving grace is that they are patiently assisting us, rather than just laughing and giving up!

Their wisdom, and insight is being channelled globally and we, as a species are waking up. We are becoming attuned to the higher reality, and stepping out of the illusion.

For this is the Age of Awakening.

The Golden Age of Aquarius, that has long been foretold and prophesied by mystics, and civilisations that are now long gone.

It cannot fail to take place. It is written in the Stars.

It is here, and it is happening now.

PART THREE

The Process of Ascension
Accessing the Higher Dimensions
Future Possibilities

Accessing the Higher Dimensions

The Process of Ascension

Inner Alchemy

Identifying Old Traits & Releasing the Past

Celestial Chakras and the Merkabah Frequency

Our Awakening and Astral Travel

Creative Visualisation & Heart Mind Harmony

The Merkabah & Sacred Geometry

The Mysterious Human DNA

Our Sovereign Heritage

Hyper-Communication

Releasing the Past & Purifying the Present

Activating Crystalline DNA

Coping with Energy Shifts

Creating the New Paradigm

Accessing The Higher Dimensions

There has been much speculation of Ascension, of shifting our frequencies from the 3rd Dimension to the 5th Dimension, and plenty of conjecture as to what that may entail.

In order to answer this we need to fully understand what Dimensions are; how many of them are there, and indeed where and how they are to be found!.

We are all very familiar with two dimensions of reality, that of dreaming and that of being awake. We may access the dream-like dimension through sleep, meditation, hypnosis, lucid dreaming, hallucinogenic drugs and many other techniques.

Every Dimension of reality has a different set of 'laws' that determine what a soul or consciousness that is in that dimension can experience. Lower dimensions are more divisive and diverse, whereas higher dimensions have frequencies of unity and oneness.

Dimensional Realms of Reality exist at the same time and occupy the same space, they are simply resonating on different vibrational frequencies of energy. We can be wide awake, and fully functioning in the physical realm, yet also experience a light trance, a day dream in the astral or etheric realms.

The structures of Time and Space are dominant features of the lower realms. Yet these phenomenon are virtually non-existent in the highest dimensions. For example, life on the Physical plane is dominated by time and space.

Our location, our time zone, and our position give us a sense of 'being' on the earth plane. Whereas, in the heavenly higher dimensions there is only Oneness, unity and connection.

Lower dimensions can be described as dense, solid, heavy and complex whereas higher dimensions can be described as light, transparent, and flexible.

We can physically only access a small fraction of the full range of frequencies that are present around us all the time.

We can access many higher realms through our Light Body, or our energy body, if it is sufficiently strong enough and prepared well enough for the journey.

When people state that they are in the 5th Dimension or higher, what they are actually referring to is their consciousness, their mind-set and their astral body frequencies.

Their physical body is blatantly still on the physical 3rd dimensional frequency but their spiritual consciousness has elevated, or ascended, into a higher state of awareness.

How Many Realms of Reality Are There?

Philosophically speaking, there are innumerable dimensions. Since we are reading this on the limited dimension of the physical plane, we can only theorise that vast realms exist beyond our current perception.

We can only see around 1% of the light spectrum. As wonderful and as colourful as the gift of sight is, on this physical plane, in this body of limitation we can only perceive 1% of what is out there! We cannot see Ultra-Violet light or, at the other end of the spectrum we cannot see Infra-Red. We only see a minute percentage of what is there! Similarly we can only conjecture that many dimensions exist. There most certainly must be many more than the 5th Dimension, which is what we are aspiring to ascend to!

We are multi-dimensional beings. Once we begin to shift our awareness, our ascension journey begins. All realms, all dimensions are accessible given the right set of circumstances.

Many of these multi-dimensional experiences occur easily and without effort or prompting on a conscious level. For example, we have all probably experienced a sense of deja vu in some way shape or form in our lifetime.

The feeling of having been somewhere before even though we are there for the first time in this life! Or meeting someone for the first time and having a distinct sense that we know them from somewhere else.

This phenomena is stretching our psyche to other dimensions. Deja vu occurs almost intuitively as we are connected with the our distant past lives. This is a typical instance of our being multi-dimensional beings, able to experience many dimensions at one time, in one space.

With practice and intention we can shift our awareness to other dimensions, and doing so can allow us to experience our daily life more purposefully. For example what we experience as a tree or a flower in our normal conscious awareness as a human on Earth, in the 3rd dimension, would have a different form and intelligence when experienced in a different dimension.

Each dimension is like a unique universe in itself, ever expanding and intermingling with its counterpart dimensional frequencies. The 3rd and 4th dimensions are very much entwined one with the other, and ascension to the 5th dimension is the next frequency.

All dimensions are accessible instantly through the astral body. Later we will look at some techniques that can assist with this process known as ascension.

We also look at how this energy shift can have an effect on our physical body as we become less carbon-based and more crystalline based structurally.

Since everything is energy, and all energy is interconnected, our ascension as a species is in true alignment with the ascension of all species, and of Gaia, Mother Earth herself.

The significance of Mother Earth can never be overlooked.

She has been abused, taken for granted, assaulted and insulted for far too long. As we ascend into the 5th dimensional frequency, we become aware of our true life purpose.

As we ascend into the 5th dimensional frequency we realise that our collective purpose as a species is that of Guardian, that of being a Custodian, a Protector.

We are designed and destined to protect and preserve Nature, to promote an harmonious state of existence here on Earth. To effectively establish Heaven on Earth.

Let us take a moment to reflect on the various dimensions.

There are many more above and beyond the frequency of the 5th Dimension, and many of us have already glimpsed these, and experienced their energies first hand.

We are essentially Multi-dimensional beings, experiencing a short temporary life of limitation on this amazing Earth Plane.

Everything is energy, and this energy is resonating at different frequencies oscillating through the various dimensions, where certain laws apply (like the laws of physics).

The 1st Dimension
This is the first level of consciousness, Everything is in a state of oneness in separation.

In order for creator to experience its own creation, it essentially required separation from its light purity.

This entails a separation from the Godhead, Creator or Source, to become manifest in a material form.

In the first dimension consciousness is pure separation, yet it is unaware of that separation. It exists, but has no individual identity. It just is.

On this dimensional frequency there is no time yet. There is no past, present or future. All things just are in that moment.

This first dimensional frequency is similar to the higher realms in its oneness, but **not** in its awareness.

We can liken this realm to the first light that shone into the chaos of darkness and created order. That order was a separation from light source of the creator.

This 1st Dimension is associated with our Root Chakra at the base of our spine.

This chakra, or vortex of energy, resonates with the frequencies of safety, security, and our basic human needs of survival.

The 1st dimension resonates with the element of the mineral kingdom. It is often also associated with the evolution of the human DNA.

The 2nd Dimension

This is the dimension of duality, and opposites. Consciousness now begins to understand that it is separate from Creator, or Source.

There is now the first notions of time as we have: now and not now.

We also have the first notions of space: this and not this.

The first notions of identity emerge: self and not self.

Time, space and identity gently come into existence through this 2nd dimensional frequency.

Life exists in this dimension with an awareness of only the present moment and its species identity.

Our own autonomic nervous system that operates to support our life without our conscious effort, is connected to the 2nd dimension.

The element associated with the 2nd dimension is associated with the water element and also associated with our Sacral Chakra located in the womb in women, representing the eternal birth of life, of ancient, modern and future civilisations.

The 3rd Dimension

This is our familiar current realm of reality. This is the Earth plane as we know it. It is here that we experience the awareness of Ego. Everything is in a distinct frequency of detachment from creator, source. It is here on the Earth plane that we also experience the incredible gift of freewill.

The 'laws' of this 3rd dimension limit the connection of oneness to all things, of all actions and all events. The past, present and future are seen as completely separate time zones, as time becomes totally linear.

This allows comparison and judgement which in turn leads to desires, goals, hopes, and fears, and the rollercoaster of a vast spectrum of emotional experiences. We begin to endure the law of karma as our thoughts, deeds, and interactions create an energy of their own.

Associated with our Solar Chakra this is the realm of self-expression,. This is the realm of desire, of an ego-lead existence resulting in polarities. These ideals of opposite belief systems result in extremely potent emotional energies. It is here on Earth that we experience, fanaticism and division in all its ugly forms: religious conflict, war, racism, hatred and cruelty.

The planet Earth is unique in the Universe in this respect. As souls incarnate here they are often amongst the most spiritually respected in all the other dimensions, as this is a realm of desire led difficulty, and distraction on all levels, physical, mental, emotional and spiritual. And we endure and often enjoy, many lifetimes on this Earth plane in the 3rd dimensional frequency. It is here that our consciousness begins to sincerely appreciate the attractions of the 4th and 5th dimensions.

Associated with the element of fire, this is often perceived to be the lowest, most dense frequency habitable, yet this is also a realm where every event is an opportunity, and the present moment is all that ever truly exists.

The 4th Dimension

This dimension operates on the frequency of thought. Thought is a potent energy.

The 4th dimension is a realm of transition, where we can experience an awakening of our spiritual consciousness. In this respect it can be seen as a necessary portal that lifts us out of the lower frequencies of the 3rd dimension and into the higher realms.

Associated with our Heart Chakra the 4th dimension is about learning the way of unconditional love. We begin to let go of the base emotions like envy, hatred, judgement and fear, and we experience an overwhelming desire for cooperation, community, connection and compassion.

Whilst we are entering the 4th Dimension we may become interested in having past life regression therapy to assist karmic release. We may also explore techniques for healing our past traumas and our inner child too.

The 4th Dimension is associated with the element of air, and our astral body. Our Astral body is our 4th dimensional self. It is also often referred to as our Energy body, our Light body, our Emotional and our Etheric body. It extends beyond our physical body and merges into our Auric Field, which stretches out beyond our skin approximately 2-6 inches.

Our Astral Body, or Light Body contains the expressions of our personality, such as our thoughts and desires, and our likes and dislikes. Our early formative traits and belief systems are also held here in the form of our Inner Child. It is through our Astral Body that we are able to function as multi-dimensional beings.

Our Astral Body also integrates what we have experienced in our 3rd Dimensional reality, and it works out the details of what we may create in our future waking reality. When we begin to understand and work with the Universal Laws of Attraction we become aware of how potent our thoughts, and words and visualisations are. It is through our Astral Body that we are able to bring our creative thoughts into manifestation.

The 5th Dimension

The 5th Dimension is the realm of Higher Thought Forms. It is in this realm that we are completely focused on spiritual awareness, and spiritual advancement of self, and all creation.

This is the dimension of our Higher Self, the realm of Spirit Guides, and Inter-Galactic Guides. Most beings in the 5th Dimension have no physical bodies. They only have Light Bodies, or put another way, they have emotional (Astral) and mental (Causal) energy bodies.

The 5th Dimension is where Higher Frequencies from Higher Dimensions can connect with our ascended consciousness. At the highest levels of the 5th Dimension, the past, present and future can all be accessed simultaneously. We can experience our many reincarnations and time-travel easily.

We have evidence of this 5th Dimensional reality already occurring on the Earth Plane as Hindu Sidhis are able to levitate their body, walk through walls and be in two places at once. These phenomena are resonant of the 5th Dimensional frequency. We also can witness Taoist practise of "nei gong" in Southeast Asia which involves the ability to start a fire with the palms of your hands, and to also use your hands as magnets.

In the 5th Dimension the oneness of everything and the unconditional love are constant experiences. The possibility of building a Utopian society, a Heaven on Earth, can only occur as we ascend into the 5th Dimension.

The 5th Dimension is associated with our Throat Chakra, the vortex of truth. We are able to freely stand in our truth and express ourselves without fear, and without judgement as these lower, restricting frequencies cannot resonate in the 5th Dimension.

The Universal Law in the 5th Dimension is the Way of Wisdom, where all creation is balanced with love.

The 6th Dimension

This dimension can be associated with our Third Eye Chakra, the eye of Insight, and Intuition. It resonates on the Spiritual plane and is about Divine Awareness.

Many beings in this dimension and higher, have never had an incarnation in a physical body. This is the dimension of the Archangels and the Ascended Masters.

Some ascended masters have experienced physical lives on Earth, for example Jesus, and St. Germain, yet some have never had a relationship with our planet.

If, or when these higher dimensional beings, the Ascended Masters, choose to incarnate on Earth, they will also face the same challenges and fears that humans in the 3rd Dimension experience.

The Ascended Masters may however, communicate with humans on the Earth plane, who have ascended to be consciously in the 5th dimensional frequency.

The overall energy of the 6th Dimension is one of a profound understanding and attunement to creator, source.

The resonance and connection to all knowledge, all understanding, all compassion.

The 7th Dimension

The 7th Dimension is the ultimate connection, and the return to the Godhead, the Source, the Creator.

We return to Oneness.

We experience an overwhelming desire to surrender to the Light.

Associated with our Crown Chakra, we find the unity that our 3rd dimensional self truly desired.

We discover the 'I am".

I am at Peace

I am

God

The First Seven Dimensions in a Nutshell

Dimension	Associated Chakra	Energy Frequency/Experiences
1st	Base Chakra	Consciousness without time/space Separation without awareness
2nd	Sacral Chakra	Duality with awareness Now/Not Now Self/Not Self
3rd	Solar Chakra	Linear Time exists: Past Present Future Karma is experienced Ego is established Self-determination Desire-led polarities resulting in judgement
4th	Heart Chakra	The Realm of Transition & Awareness Astral Body assisting spiritual awakening Self-healing techniques
5th	Throat Chakra	Higher Self & Realm of Spirit Guides Awareness of Cosmic Truth The Way of Wisdom
6th	Third Eye Chakra	Spiritual Plane - Ascended Masters

		Knowledge, Compassion & Understanding
7th	Crown Chakra	Oneness I am I am at Peace I am God

The Process of Ascension

Ascension does not mean that we are going to suddenly drift off into another zone, another World, as tempting as that might sound at times!

The process of our Ascension as a species, and as individuals, refers to the rising of our conscious awareness.

We access the ascension process as we expand our consciousness into heart-based enlightenment, living in a state of grace, love, compassion and co-operation.

It isn't an easy or comfortable process, letting go of long-held beliefs. We have been misled and conditioned to resonate in a constant state of division, competition, fear, and confusion.

Happily, those days are coming to an end. The awakening is well underway now. It has been long foretold and prophesied by our forebears, by civilisations long gone, and by the planetary orbits and inter-galactic beings. This is the prophesied Golden Age, an age of enlightenment, freedom and compassion.

What do we need to do to join in?
How is it going to affect us as individuals and as a civilisation?
What happens now?

As humans, experiencing a short life of limitation on this physical plane of Earth bound energy, we have been granted the gift of free will. This is an incredible gift of love.

We are essentially free to choose to embrace ascension, and we are also free to choose to continue in an ego-led life of indulgence, self-interest, and greed.

As we are each individually responsible for our own enlightenment, so we must respect the path chosen by others. Everyone is treading a unique pathway, no two journeys will ever be identical. There will be similarities, and common experiences, but each soul's ascension is original, a singular return to the All That Is.

Inner Alchemy

When we think of Alchemy we are usually drawn to the ancient tale of the search for the recipe of turning common base metal into valuable gold. Inner alchemy is exactly that.

The pathway of Ascension involves deciphering the recipe for turning our inner base energy into valuable golden light.

This inner alchemy takes many shapes and forms. First and foremost is an understanding of the rules. An understanding and an appreciation of the 'Universal Laws' that govern life on this physical plane and the realms beyond.

All realms are bound by certain frequencies or 'Universal Laws' that hold that frequency in it's realm of being.

For example, on the 3rd Dimensional Earth Plane we have the laws of Time, Karma, Manifestation, and Free Will.

In the 3rd dimension we are led by ego, by self-interest and the search for validation.

Our words, our thoughts and actions in this 3rd dimensional frequency may often be critical, rude, hurtful to others, and to ourselves, as they are driven by ego. The 3rd dimension was desire-led, experience-led, ego-led.

The 3rd dimension is resonant with the Solar Plexus Chakra in our physical body.

It is the 4th dimensional energies that awaken us to the effect our words, thoughts and actions have had. We may become aware that we really do 'reap what we sow', that karma really is a thing!

Resonant with our Heart Chakra in our physical body the 4th dimension is a learning curve!

We are open to understanding that for every action is a reaction, that like attracts like, and that everything is energy in a constant state of impermanence and change.

We begin to find ourselves drawn to the right teacher at the right time, or we stumble as if by coincidence across the right book, or video that totally shifts our understanding and our perception of reality thus far.

It is in a 4th dimensional state that our hearts begin to open to the wonder of life, to the higher realms of reality. And so we move into a higher state of being. The 5th dimension.

In the 5th dimensional state of conscious awareness, we are careful and mindful of our every thought, word and deed.

This 5th dimension resonates with our Throat Chakra, the vortex of Truth. We comprehend intuitively. We are fully attuned to our higher self and practice living in a loving state of grace as fully as possible.

We have endured thousands of years of misrule, misinformation and manipulation.
We have forgotten who we really are, that we are essentially multi-dimensional spiritual beings.

Each and every one of us is Creator incarnate.

It is the remembering of this essential truth that brings enlightenment, inner peace and ascension.

Through the vital return journey home to Creator, we surrender to the Light that Is.

The first dimensional energy is Creator creating.

The second dimensional energy is Creator separating in order to experience its creation.

The third dimensional energy is Creator surrendering to freewill, to the expansion of ego.

The fourth dimensional energy is Creator searching for clarity and an understanding of it's creation, and to experience the journey home.

The fifth dimensional energy is Creator on that journey home, leading on to the wondrous re-creation of Oneness.

Awareness of the these Universal Laws will assist us as we later use Creative Visualisation techniques that enable us to shift our energy and our consciousness, through the 4th Dimension and into the 5th Dimensional Consciousness.

The Universal Laws of Attraction on 3rd Dimension

1. Energy of Attraction Thought-Word-Emotion-Action	POWER
2. Law of Opposites In the absence of that which you are not, that which you are, is not. i.e. Hot without Cold, is not Hot. As soon as we invoke the Energy of Attraction, we activate the Law of Opposites. If we are not vigilant we could be discouraged and see this as a 'sign' or 'omen' that things are not to be. Work through the Law of Opposites. Stay focussed.	OPPORTUNITY
3. Gift of Wisdom This gift allows us to distinguish between both of the above principles. Maintain the mindset: 'The best outcome for me is coming now.'	DISCERNMENT

Failure is a blessing in disguise as it presents an opportunity to succeed. Through wisdom we discern all reality is an illusion.	
4. Joy of Wonder Our natural state and purpose is to experience all the 'wonder' of Life. We are co-creators using our rich imagination.	IMAGINATION
5. Presence of Cycles There are no straight lines. Eventually everything meets itself. We have forever/infinity to experience our desires. This awareness presents us with the gift of patience. We become aware of the importance of Trusting The Process of Life.	ETERNAL SOUL ENERGY

Inner Alchemy transmutes our base self into connection with our Higher Self.

Our Higher Self is essentially the part of us that is not controlled by ego. It is that spiritual part of us that is connected to All That Is, the cosmic or celestial whole. Our Higher Self is aligned with the 5th dimension and higher.

It is here that we find we are able to connect with our Spirit Guides, those patient, loving entities that wait for our fractured light to become whole once again.

To become whole once again, we are committed to releasing the past ties to the 3rd dimension, those of fear, judgement, criticism and the like. We release all karma, through past life regression work and inner child healing.

Inner Alchemy Techniques

Past Life Regression   Inner Child Healing

Reiki Healing   Astral Travel

Forgiveness   Mindfulness

Hypnotherapy   Creative Visualisation

Positive Affirmations   Journalling / Channelling

Meditation   Yoga

Tai Chi/ QiGong   Self-healing

Identifying Old Traits & Releasing the Past

Our bodies are undergoing great change during this particular moment in time.

Old karmic ties are being severed so that our bodies can absorb and radiate more light.
As we release the shadows of the past we allow space for new higher frequencies to move throughout our psyche.

When we have released the past and let go of old habits, regrets, and traits that have held us back for so long, we are able to make space for higher light frequencies that have a superior vibration to those previously experienced here on Earth.

These higher frequencies are able to access and develop our physical body through what scientist had previously labelled 'junk DNA'. Scientist and researchers now know that only 10% of our DNA is used for building proteins. The other 90% they considered "junk DNA. This Junk is now coming into its own, as its true purpose is being realised. Later we explore some fascinating research and offer invaluable techniques for activating our ascended crystalline DNA.

Everything is comprised of energy, and this energy is in a constant state of impermanence and change. Our DNA is not exempt from this universal law. Our DNA is now in a state of inner alchemy, of inner ascension.

The new light rays have new signature patterns that help us to clear old blockages. These new light rays are illuminating exactly what we need to identify and release.

For example we may experience many ego-based negative forces which are now coming to the surface for release. These blockages may manifest in a variety of ways.

We may experience some or all of the following:

lack of self-worth	fear and anger	anxiety
depression	restlessness	confusion and doubt
attachment to negative energy	exhaustion and lethargy	recurring dreams
sleep disturbance	tinnitus (ringing in the ears)	sadness and regret

These profound emotional energies are surfacing now. They are surfacing now because they are no longer of use as our energies alchemise and ascend. They are part of our old 3rd dimensional experience.

The Ego-led life that produced these limiting and restricting emotional energies, is no longer required as we advance and upgrade our DNA, our psyche and our species as a whole.

As we release old karmic ties and imprints, our vibration will become lighter as we move via the 4th dimensional awareness programme towards the 5th dimension, and the blissful acceptance of The Cosmic Truth.

As we integrate the new light frequencies their new signature patterns will also shift our essence on a physical level. We may also experience physical aches and pains as our body responds accordingly.

For example, we may experience some or all of the following symptoms:

aching joints	heightened sensitivity to sound and light
blurred vision	muscle cramps
dizziness	flu-like symptoms
brain fog	heart palpitations

As the intensity of the incoming light frequencies rises, we may well loose sight of the progress we are actually making. Progress in our own individual psyche, and progress for all humanity.

This is an excellent time to begin journalling our experiences. Keeping a personal record helps us to see just how far we have come.

A diary of our ascension encourages us, since we are then creating an opportunity look back at how much courageous change has been made.

We can remind ourselves just how vast an energy shift we have endured and how we have successfully transformed from base metal into gold, from base energy into light!

Part of the process is that we must cleanse and eliminate the toxins that have built up over many lifetimes. And this is being done on a global, and planetary scale too. Mother Earth is shifting in her own energetic paradigm.

The solar flares that are helping us to upgrade our DNA, and shift our vibrational frequency also impact on our Earth too.

The Schumann Resonance has never been more fluctuating and active since records began. Whilst this increase heightens our sensitivities, especially to light and sound, so too it impacts on the plant, animal and mineral realms.

Everything is energy, and everything is in a state of impermanence and change.

Any symptoms that we may experience will clear as our natural energy frequency continues to ascend, and we realise the urgency in releasing any energy blocks or old emotional ties, and negative thought patterns.

Our physical body is a temporary housing for our powerful, and eternal Light Spirit.

As we let go of the 3rd dimensional fears, as we see through the lies and limitations of the past, so our spirit shines into the space vacated by the shadows of dis-ease and discomfort and despair.

We also begin to bring dormant extra-sensory abilities into play. These portals of communication with the higher realms, previously undeveloped and unused, now begin to activate.

As our energy is purified on all levels, spiritual, emotional, psychological and physical, so our sixth senses, our extra-sensory skills, become empowered and accessible to us.

This opens new insights, and new downloads of otherwise untapped information.

As we, as a species, become more enlightened, as we quite naturally evolve and embrace the new energies of the 5th dimension, so we also become more connected to each other.

As the energy of conflict, and competition erodes away, the blessings of compassion and cooperation will be experienced.

Celestial Chakras & Merkabah Frequency

We can literally study the phenomenon of Chakras for an entire lifetime and still not conclude the entirety of all that has been written on the subject.

A chakra is the common term for a vortex of energy. The chakras are energy points on living body and in its auric field that transmit life-force energy into the physical body. Acupuncture uses the system of meridians, or energy lines, that stem from the chakra system.

Our light-body, our aura and our chakra system is vital to sustain our physical body.

We have many thousands of chakras in our physical body and in our metaphysical auric field. Generally most people are aware of the seven major chakras that correspond to the seven colours of the light spectrum, and the seven notes of the musical scale.

We are now going to explore the developing chakras in our light-body, in our auric field and our auric light-column.

Each chakra has an overall theme, or purpose. Some teachers indicate that chakras must turn in a specific way, clockwise or anticlockwise, others that the speed of the chakra must be of a specific rhythm in order to align harmoniously with the other chakras.

My personal philosophy, and the teachings that I have received, is that each of us is genuinely unique, and we will each experience the 4th and 5th dimensional chakras in a deeply personal way.

A GUIDE TO
The 22 Chakra System
& 3rd - 5th Dimensional Shift

3rd Dimensional Chakras: ego-led - found in physical body

1. ROOT CHAKRA	BASE OF SPINE	RED
2. SACRAL CHAKRA	LOWER ABDOMEN	ORANGE
3. SOLAR PLEXUS	UPPER ABDOMEN	YELLOW
4. HEART	CENTRE OF CHEST	GREEN/PINK
5. THROAT	NECK	SKY BLUE
6. THIRD EYE	FOREHEAD	INDIGO BLUE
7. CROWN	TOP OF HEAD	VIOLET/WHITE

4th Dimensional Chakras: awareness-led - found in auric field

8. EARTH STAR	6" BELOW FEET	SILVER/RED
9. HIGHER HEART	THORAX	TURQUOISE
10. ALTA MAJOR	BACK OF NECK	PEARLESCENT
11. CAUSAL	BACK OF CROWN	BLUE/WHITE
12. SOUL STAR	6" ABOVE CROWN	VIOLET/PINK
13. SPIRIT STAR	6" BEHIND SOUL STAR	INDIGO/PINK

14. COSMIC STAR	6" ABOVE SOUL STAR	TURQUOISE/PINK
15. STELLA GATEWAY	18" ABOVE CROWN	PLATINUM/PINK

5th Dimensional Chakras: consciousness-led - in auric light column

16. STAR CHILD	AURIC LIGHT COLUMN	VIOLET/BLUE
17. SOLAR STAR	""	MAGENTA
18. GALACTIC STAR	""	WHITE/GOLD
19. UNIVERSAL MOTHER	""	PINK/GOLD
20. UNIVERSAL FATHER	""	BLUE/GOLD
21. UNIVERSAL SUN	""	VIOLET/GOLD
22. DIVINE GATEWAY	""	GOLD

Chakras are vortexes of energy, light energy.

They are receivers and transformers of light energy and it is through the chakra system that we absorb the vital life force energy that sustains our physical, mental, emotional and spiritual energy bodies.

This vital life force energy is recognised in ancient spiritual modalities, yoga, reiki, tai chi and qigong and acupuncture to name just a few.

Science is always proving what spiritual teachers have always known! Scientists study the fascinating brainwaves and electromagnetic activity in the body. Our body is comprised of trillions and trillions of atoms, and science teaches us that atoms are 99.9% light. These atoms are resonating on different frequencies, and the chakra system keeps those light waves of life-sustaining energy in harmonious alignment for optimum health and vibrancy.

If a chakra is blocked or if it is resonating at an imperfect frequency contrary to its true function, then we begin to experience the consequences of this discord, as it begins to manifest from our light body to resonate in our physical body as dis-ease.

There are many more chakras than the 22 we have identified. We have thousands of chakras that vary in significance, function and size. There are internal chakras in our inner organs, there are many on the palms of our hands and on the soles of our feet.

It could easily become a lifetimes work to study all the chakras that exist. Just as we began with the realisation of the 7 major chakras when we first became spiritually inquisitive, so we now focus on the ascending chakras, the 22 chakras of the 4th and 5th Dimension.

Since the inception of the 4th dimension and the onset of the Age of Aquarius, back in the 1960's and '70's, the ayurvedic arts, yoga, reiki and tai chi, have thrived and blossomed, becoming mainstream. With their wisdom, came the knowledge and acceptance of the chakra system. The seven major chakras all resonate on the 3rd dimensional frequency, being ego-based and ego-led.

The Seven Major Chakras
- 3rd Dimension

1. The Root Chakra - sits at the very base of our spine. It resonates to the colour Ruby Red. It is where we connect with our primal instincts of survival: safety, money, food, security. It is where we become grounded.

2. The Sacral Chakra - is located a few inches below our belly button. The colour associated with this chakra is Orange. It is the place of creativity and pleasure. Our sexuality is connected to this power house too. This is where we connect with our emotions and where we interact emotionally with others.

3. The Solar Chakra - is Sunshine Yellow. It is found just above the belly button. This is, as it name suggests, the powerhouse of our energy. It is here we connect with our self, with our self-confidence, self-approval and self-acceptance.

4. The Heart Chakra - this beautiful chakra is found in the heart area in the very centre of our chest. It resonates on the colour ray of Green. This is where we connect with love. When we open our heart chakra we experience the ecstasy of pure unconditional Love.
We touch the Divine within and find inner peace, and joy.

5. The Throat Chakra - resonates on a clear Sky Blue colour. This is the chakra of communication. Here we connect with hearing as well as speaking. It is where we find Truth.

6. Third Eye Chakra - is located between our eyebrows, in the temple of our fore-head. It's colour is Indigo, deep inky Blue. It is the centre of intuition, where we ignite our imagination, where we see clearly when we are enlightened.

7. The Crown Chakra - This is found, as it's name implies, on the top of our head. It is the fastest vibrating chakra of the seven majors, and is a vivid ultra Violet colour. It is here we connect to The Divine. When our major chakras have an imbalance they cannot function properly and our physical body experiences dis-ease in some way, shape of form.

Some of the following list suggestions as to how this imbalance may occur:

HEAD   Separation from Divine or True Self

BACK   Out of alignment with life. An inability to accept support from family and friends.

THROAT   Not living our true self. Too much compromising.

LOWER BACK   Financial worry. Concerns about security and the future.

SHOULDERS   Taking on too much responsibility. Conflict with progress.

SOLAR PLEXUS   Low self-esteem, poor self-worth, little self-confidence.

STOMACH   Trouble digesting ideas.

BREAST   Inability to be nurturing to self and others.

LEGS   Making quick decisions. Reacting too fast.

KNEES   Reluctance to admit fear. Insecure and low self-esteem.

SHINS   Fear of the future.

ANKLES   Separation from nature and feminine.

Of course these are simply suggestions. There are other explanations for chakras to be operating in a dysfunctional way.

There may be a cord of attachment, to a person, place or thing, that is creating an energy leak in the auric field.

There may be a trauma or injustice from a past life that is manifesting as an irrational fear or phobia that needs to be reprocessed and released before any ascension or progress can occur.

Similarly there may be an imbalance in the Karma that an individual has built up over many incarnations.

It may also be that the personality, the ego, has developed unhealthy mindsets, perhaps of criticism, anger, hatred, and greed.

All these imbalances must be addressed before the individual can work through the 4th Dimension and on to the 5th Dimension.

Healing modalities like past life regression, reiki healing, crystal healing, inner child work and other holistic healing processes are invaluable at this stage. They are specifically designed to realign any negative energies, and release and reprocess any blocked emotional and karmic ties.

We can also help ourselves by listening to our body as it gently whispers to us.

If we feel an ache, a pain, a stiffness that is restricting our lifestyle, it pay to tune into it and speak to it gently, and lovingly. Rather than stuffing a pain-killer down our neck, and telling our ethereal body to literally "shut up", it is far more advantageous to listen to what it is asking you to do to help and heal the dis-ease.

Often times small, simple changes to our lifestyle, our diet, and our mindset result in amazing healing, a lifting of the old ways and an embracing of the new. Shifting the base matter into new light. Alchemising our energy.

We can attune to our seven major chakras in an effort to keep them healthy.

The seven major chakras are all based in our physical body. They all resonate on the ego-led 3rd Dimension.

When our chakras are fully enlightened, free from dis-ease and discord, then we can embrace the higher dimensions and work on strengthening the rest of our light body so it can carry us forward into the long foretold process of Ascension.

How To Keep The Seven Major Chakras Healthy

Crown Chakra:
Ask yourself: Am I open to Spirit and my Higher Self?
Possible Problems: Disturbed sleep. Feeling disconnected from your body. Difficulty concentrating or meditating.
Solutions: Sunlight. Walks in nature, or gardening. Connect with Trees.
Affirmations: I AM AT PEACE IN THE WONDERS OF NATURE.

Third Eye Chakra:
Ask yourself: What do I want to visualise?
Possible Problems: Depression. Poor eyesight. Lack of intuition. Hormonal imbalance.
Solutions: Add the following into your diet: Blackberries, Plums, Purple Grapes or Purple Grape Juice.
Affirmations: THE FUTURE LOOKS BRIGHT AND PROMISING.

Throat Chakra:
Ask yourself: Are there any issues that I need to resolve?
Possible Problems: Frequent sore throat. Difficulty expressing emotions. Thyroid problems.
Solutions: Add the following into your diet: Blueberries, Raspberries, Figs, Kelp.
Affirmations: I EXPRESS MYSELF FREELY AND JOYOUSLY.

Heart Chakra:
Ask yourself: Is my heart open?

Possible Problems: Heart and Lung problems. Asthma. Allergies. Fear of intimacy.
Solutions: Add the following into your diet: Broccoli, Kale, Chard, any other leafy greens.
Affirmations: MY HEART IS FULL OF LOVE

Solar Plexus Chakra:
Ask yourself: Am I balanced in my personality?
Possible Problems: Bloating. Liver Problems. Stomach ulcers. Eating disorders. Excessive gas. Lack of confidence. Procrastination.
Solutions: Add the following into your diet: Bananas, Yellow peppers, Yellow Lentils ,Oats, Sweet Corn.
Affirmations: I SEE POSSITIVITY AND JOY EVERYWHERE.

Sacral Chakra:
Ask yourself: Am I centered?
Possible Problems: Hip pain. Infertility. Sexual problems. Emotional imbalance. Creative blockages.
Solutions: Add the following into your diet: Oranges, Seeds, Nuts, Carrots, Pumpkins.
Affirmations: I AM IN PERFECT BALANCE WITH LIFE.

Root Chakra:
Ask yourself: Am I grounded?
Possible Problems: Lower Back pain. Colon problems. Varicose veins. Emotional issues connected to security and finance.
Solutions: Add the following into your diet: Beetroot, Parsnips, Apples, Pomegranates, any form of additional protein.
Affirmations: I TRUST THE PROCESS OF LIFE. I AM SAFE.

We can also embrace meditation techniques with a view to balancing the energy in our seven major chakras.

Meditation Script for Cleansing the Aura and Balancing the Chakras of the 3rd Dimension

Finding yourself in a nice comfortable position, just relax totally, and without trying, gently become aware of your breathing ~
Notice the energy that you feel as you breathe.
Feel it entering your body.
Concentrate on that gentle sensation as it enters your nostrils.
Just allow the energy to flow gently ~
And breathing in compassion and unconditional love.
And breathing out nurturing love for everything.
Breathing in compassion and unconditional love ~ and breathing out nurturing love for everything.

As you breathe in this unconditional love energy you are totally aware that you too, are energy itself ~ that it flows through you every moment of every day.

Breathe in this beautiful energy into your root chakra, at your pelvis.
As you exhale breathe out any tension that is held in the spine.
Visualise a beautiful glowing red gem-like quality pulsating in your pelvis.
See it sparkle as it turns ~ so bright, like a beautiful Red ruby ~

Feel patience and security, as you breathe energy into this red root chakra.
And as you exhale let go of any tension that is held in your spine or legs ~
Relax totally ~
Visualise this red sparkling sphere settling into perfect harmonious alignment in your pelvis ~ a glowing ruby Red orb ~
And bless it with unconditional love ~

Once again, gently focus on your breathing ~ move your awareness to the sacral chakra just below your naval.
Imagine a beautiful Orange orb ~ Breathe unconditional love into this energy ~
Release any feelings of over-indulgence or possession ~ let go of any emotional desire ~
Visualise this orange sphere spinning a little faster and becoming brighter as if a light has been switched on inside it ~
Feel warmth and harmonious health within ~
Picture both Red and Orange orbs are the same size ~ the orange spinning a little faster than the red ~
And bless it with pure unconditional love ~

Once again, gently return your focus to your breathing ~ move your awareness to the solar plexus, just above your naval.
Imagine a glowing Golden Yellow orb ~ Breathe pure unconditional love into this energy ~
Feel radiance and warmth like Sunshine contained within ~
As you breathe out let go of fear or any stored anger ~ just let it go
Breathe in positive energy to nurture yourself ~

See all negativity disappearing as the chakra shines and glows like the Sun ~
Again visualise the Golden Yellow Sunshine orb the same size as the two below only
spinning a little faster ~ clean ~ bright ~
and bless it with pure unconditional love

Focus on your breath again ~ and move your awareness to the Heart ~
Think of the beautiful energy there ~ breathe pure unconditional love into your heart ~
envisage this orb of bright Green energy spinning pure and bright ~
Let go of any blocked emotions ~
feel the release of any weight or heaviness in the heart, as it becomes lighter and lighter ~
See any unwanted energy from this green energy centre, flowing away from your body to be re-seeded in the earth ~ back to nature ~
see any shadows dissipate as your heart energy shines like sunshine on a Green emerald ~ feel compassion ~ and forgiveness ~ and love for all things ~
again, visualise this orb of energy the same size as those below ~
the Yellow solar ~
the Orange sacral ~
the Red root ~
and each one vibrating a little faster than those below ~

Breathe in compassion and unconditional love ~
Breathe out nurturing love for all things ~

Move your focus to your throat chakra ~
as you breathe in the pure energy that is Life ~

breathe it into your throat chakra ~ see a beautiful Sky Blue
~ deep and tranquil ~
allow any negative thoughts to float away ~ like dark clouds
~ leaving behind only a clear blue sky ~
breathe in gentleness ~
breathe in truth ~ and kindness ~
see this beautiful clear Blue energy on a higher vibrational field than the heart ~
spinning with purity and truth and gentleness ~
breathing in unconditional love and compassion once again,
feeling calm and relaxed ~

move your attention to the velvet Indigo energy that dwells in your temple, behind your eyes ~
feel this energy as it brings with it peace of mind and wisdom ~
release any fears and worries ~ let go of any troubles ~ or any bad dreams ~
allow this deep dark Indigo-Blue energy to soothe and caress your mind as you relax deeper and deeper ~
breathe pure unconditional love into this temple ~
visualise this energy-sphere the same size as the others, only turning a little faster ~ soothing ~ safe ~ pure ~ peaceful ~

focus again on your breathing ~ feeing so calm and relaxed ~

gently become aware of the crown chakra ~ a magnificent Magenta colour ~
it spins the fastest of all the chakras ~ like a crown on top of your head ~
as you sense this orb of bright Violet-Purple energy imagine all hesitation being released ~

connect with a feeling of selflessness ~
attune yourself to your Higher Self ~ to this beautiful selfless love energy ~
all knowing ~ all nurturing ~ accept the feeling and knowledge that you are eternal ~
that you are God-Energy ~ Invincible ~ Infinite ~ Eternal ~

See this chakra in your imagination as it vibrates on the highest level
faster than of all the other chakras~
bright ~ clean ~ energising ~

and you can see all the chakras below ~
acknowledge their different colours ~
their different vibrations ~
their different qualities and gifts ~

journey through the crown magnificent and sacred ~ a vibrant Purple-Violet,
the Indigo temple ~
the Sky-Blue throat ~
the Emerald-Green heart ~
feel the Golden Sunshine warmth in the solar plexus ~
and the comforting Orange below it ~
and finally the Red-Ruby root chakra ~

Your light body ~ perfect ~ cleansed ~ balanced and at one with all that is ~

Surround yourself now with a sparkling Silver light ~
that creates a safe halo all around your being ~
creating a shimmering protection of light ~
and this silver energy is shielded by a further halo of Sacred Golden Energy ~

vibrations from the Divine ~
and this Light is an Eternal Light ~
it is always present and always there ~
it permeates the material ~
protecting and nurturing ~
Invincible and Infinite ~
it brings Security, and Peace and Harmony ~
it brings Laughter, Compassion and Truth ~
It bring Wisdom and Awareness that you are All ~
and also part of all that is ~
that You are One with the Creator ~

Bring your awareness back to your breathing ~
breathing in love and compassion ~
breathing out love for all things ~
Breathing in beautiful bliss ~
Blessing all things as you exhale ~

And bringing your awareness back to the present moment ~

gently open your eyes ~

It is a good idea to record the above, (pausing at the symbol ~), so that you can listen to it several times. Our subconscious mind loves repetition and it it is no secret that advertising agents know exactly how to get into our brain, through repetition and suggestion.

Rather than succumbing to their devious mind control techniques, it is far more empowering to take control of the situation and create our own healing, positive brainwaves.

Lets take a look at the newly emerging celestial chakras that are found in our auric field.

Numbered 8-15 they resonate on the 4th Dimension and are awareness led. They are essential to the healthy structure of our Light Body. We need this Light Body to be fully functional when we access the 5th Dimension where more ethereal chakras evolve.

These chakras are essential to our ascension process. Imagine them in the auric field like a light strand of DNA. They swirl and spiral through our aura sometimes moving closer to our physical body and sometimes expanding into our Merkabah and our Auric Light Column, which we explore in greater detail soon.

As we ascend in consciousness our personal understanding of the potential vastness of our energy system is quite literally mind blowing. We may experience some of these celestial chakras more than others.

Some may be more pertinent to us than others. The best thing we can do is to relax and enjoy the process. Trust in the knowledge that you are guided for your highest good at all times.

Training our ego to be still and calm is one of the greatest challenges, and once we have mastered that, we can then begin to enjoy the ride.

The great paradox: in order to ascend we must first descend. We must first attune to the Earth Star vortex which anchors and protects our light body at all times.

Just as our root chakra protects our physical energy, creating security, so the Earth Star protects our Light Body through the vast Auric Field.

4th Dimensional Chakras

8. The Earth Star
A sphere located 6" beneath the feet.
Dull/Invisible when dormant. Silver/Red when awakened
Awakens profound environmental awareness
Bloodstone, Obsidian, Hematite
Affirmation "I am open to the great mystery of life"

9. The Higher Heart
Located at the Thorax and in the body and the auric field
Turquoise, Chrysocolla,
Awakens us to Discernment
Vivid Turquoise
Affirmation "I stand in my truth with strength"

10. The Alta Major
Located at the back of the neck moves from aura to body
Pearlescent
Assists balance and release of Karma
Aqua Aura, Moonstone, Milky Quartz
Affirmation "I release all fear. I am at peace with myself."

11. The Causal Chakra
Positioned 10cm behind the Crown Chakra
White / Blue in colour
Encourages action and channels guidance
Clear Quartz, Herkimer Diamond,
Affirmation "I release all burdens and I cherish my insights"

12. The Soul Star Chakra
Located 6" above the Crown Chakra
Peach/Pink
Opens to Soul awareness. Life purpose
Opal or Pink Tourmaline
Affirmation "My life journey is always a beginning"

13. Spirit Star Chakra
Located 6" behind Soul Star
Indigo/Pink
Assists intuition. Connection to acquired past life virtues.
Kunsite
Affirmation "I am at peace with who I am."

14. Cosmic Star Chakra
Located 6" above Soul Star
Turquoise / Pink
Stimulates DNA Accesses light codes and functions.
Pink Turquoise
Affirmation "I relax and accept all that exists."

15. The Stellar Gateway Chakra
Positioned 18"above the Crown Chakra
Platinum/Pink
Connects to The 5th Dimension and Higher Realms
Moldavite
Affirmation "I am a spark of all creation. I am God"

The Chakras of the 4th dimension ground our celestial light body through the Earth Star.

Our Light Column is developing in our auric field and getting stronger with each specific enlightened thought, word, and deed.

Our frequency is manifesting in the light, and the light frequency is teaching us and raising our consciousness moment by moment.

Meditation to attune to the 4th Dimensional Chakras

Finding yourself in a nice comfortable position, just relax totally, and without trying, gently become aware of your breathing ~
Notice the energy that you feel as you breathe.
Feel it entering your body.
Concentrate on that gentle sensation as it enters your nostrils.
Just allow the energy to flow gently ~
And breathing in compassion and unconditional love.
And breathing out nurturing love for everything.
Breathing in compassion and unconditional love ~ and breathing out nurturing love for everything.

As you breathe in this unconditional love energy you are totally aware that you too, are energy itself ~ that it flows through you every moment of every day.

Allow your imagination to guide you to float through your seven major chakras
begin with the Crown.

Visualise the Light floating through your Crown and harmonising the energy there in a loving light haze of gold, silver and violet ~

This Light now shines behind the Third Eye, illuminating your insight and intuition in wave of indigo light ~

Flowing further now the Light shines through your throat, a brilliant sky blue allow yourself to feel relaxed and at peace ~

As now this wave of Light energy flows down to your Heart chakra, sensing a wonderful feeling of peace and tranquility ~ a beautiful glowing green frequency ~
allow the soft petals of your heart to gently open in compassion and unconditional love,

As this wave of eternal Light energy now flows to your solar plexus ~ instilling a feeling of happiness and joy with a sparkling bright yellow brilliance ~

Flowing further to the sacral chakra and the light attunes to a warm orange light ~
feel the energy of perfection, harmony, safety, trust ~

As now the Light flows to the root chakra at the base of spine ~ a sensation of strength and power glow like a powerful red fire ball ~

Visualising all the seven power points alight, alive and free ~ as the Light flows further now beyond your feet and into the Earth to align with your Earth Star Chakra ~

As the Light connects to your Earth Star Chakra the soles of your feet begin to tingle as they are transforming the frequency of your Light Column into Mother Earth ~

Visualise the Light flowing in a silver/red frequency becoming metallic as it resonates in your Earth Star Chakra ~ allow a moment to linger here ~ basking in the strength and tranquility of your Earth Star Chakra ~ your breath is slow and at peace ~ just flowing ~

The Light now guides you to shift to the counter balancing chakra ~ as you sense the resonance of your Soul Star Chakra above your Crown ~ At the speed of light you are there ~ at your Soul Star Chakra above your Crown ~

You can see the shapes of your Auric Light Column ascending above like a Light show of bright iridescent ribbons and orbs ~ each emitting love and more love and you feel this love in your heart ~

As you resonate in your Soul Star Light basking in a violet/pink frequency of compassion and love ~ you sense behind you the indigo/pink of your Spirit Star Chakra ~ sensing a wonderful wave of security, protection and understanding ~

Above your Soul Star Chakra you are able to connect to two higher Light centres ~
your Cosmic Star shining like an opal, pink and turquoise ~ emitting a sense of acceptance, peace and humility ~

And higher still you perceive your Stella Gateway ~ a wide frequency of platinum/pink love welcoming and embracing your psyche ~ your heart is full of love ~ your mind is enlightened with love ~

As now your are guided to look down your Light Column from the position of your Stella Gateway ~ your Light Body is strengthening ~ shining brighter ~ shining stronger every moment of every day ~

as now you float down the iridescent kaleidoscope ~ through your Cosmic Star and Spirit Star ~ as you settle in you Soul Star above your Crown ~

Become aware of your blue/white Causal Chakra behind your Crown ~ you float down to this frequency ~ basking in the Light ~ you bless your insight as you also sense the urge to release any fears that block your way ~

The lighter your burdens ~ the stronger your Light Body can ascend ~ as each time you bring light to this Chakra ~ so it shines brighter and closer to your physical body ~ you take a moment to linger here ~ experiencing your Light Body as if for the first time ~

The Light now guides you to your Alta Major at the back of the neck as it resonates in a beautiful pearlescent light ~ you are embraced in a loving frequency of peace and tranquility ~ as you attune to this frequency this chakra becomes clearer and brighter as all fears that block your way are released ~ you have no fear ~ for you are Light ~

This realisation sparks the turquoise light in your Higher Heart Chakra to become vibrant as it flows too and from your aura and your physical body ~ an infinite wave of truth, discernment and strength ~

Your Light shines into your heart ~ your beautiful heart ~ your centre of Infinite Love and Light ~ as you see yourself as you truly are ~ LIGHT

You see and sense the light chakras above and below in a Light Column of Iridescent Light waves ~ emanating from wonderful orbs of Light in your chakras ~

Your heart resonates with the Source of Light, eager to experience more ~ grateful for the experience thus far ~

the yin and the yang ~ the inner and the outer ~ as above so below ~

You become aware of your breath ~ your in breath ~ your out breath ~
Your intuition is preparing you to return to the here and now ~ the present moment ~

You seal your Light Body in the protective Egg-shell Shaped Golden Shield of Light ~

Breathing in and cherishing yourself ~
Breathing our and cherishing all creation ~

Bringing your awareness back to the present moment and when you 're ready open your eyes ~ and smile !

Our Awakening

We are multidimensional beings.

This truth becomes clear during our awakening which is guided by the activation of these 4th dimensional chakras, these wonderful vortexes of bright light vibration.

When we study the 3rd dimensional chakras, (the major seven chakras), we locate them specifically in the physical body. When we are working with the 4th and 5th dimensional chakras, we are working in our Light Body, also known as our auric field. This is the realm of vibration and fractured light frequency.

Lets imagine a beautiful window crystal that is designed to refract sunlight and create spectrumatic patterns of light around the room. This is evidence that pure clear light is, in fact, multidimensional. The clear light is composed of many bright and vibrant colours.

Our Light Body is composed of many bright and vibrant frequencies all resonating simultaneously at different vibrations . This Light Body is coloured by our Conscious Thought Awareness. Our thoughts, and our consciousness create our vibrational frequency and therefore our reality, and ultimately our experiences.

As these auric chakras become stronger, they will expand and strengthen our Merkabah shield, and bring this Light into our consciousness too. We shall explore this phenomenon in the next few pages.

These intensely powerful geometrical light patterns enable our Conscious Thought Awareness to rise beyond the 5th dimension.

5th Dimensional Chakras: consciousness-led – in auric light column

16. Star Child
Located in the Auric Light Column beyond Stella Gateway
Violet/ Blue
Awareness "I am a loving child of the Universe"

17. Solar Star
Located in the Auric Light Column beyond the Star Child
Magenta
Awareness "I am more than I experience."

18. Galactic Star
Located in the Auric Light Column beyond the Solar Star
White/Gold
Awareness "I belong to everything, everywhere, always"

19. Universal Mother
In Auric Light Column beyond the Galactic Star
Pink/Gold
Awareness "I love and I am loved. I create and I experience."

20. Universal Father
In Auric Light Column beside Universal Mother
Blue/Gold
Awareness "I love and I am loved. I protect and nurture creation."

21. Universal Sun
In Auric Light Column beyond Universal Mother/Father Violet/Gold
Awareness "I am safe in the Light. I am the Light.'

22. Divine Gateway
In Auric Light Column before it opens and expands. Gold
Awareness "I surrender myself."

These Higher Celestial Chakras can be accessed simultaneously, at the same time. This may occur for what may appear to be a fleeting moment in time on this physical 3rd dimensional level. Sometimes we may have very little mental recognition of the actual experience and at other times the occurrence is vivid and blissfully memorable.

When we attune to the higher realms and our Light Body strengthens, we may experience moments of pure ecstasy and bliss. These teasing tasters encourage us to keep coming back for more. Our hunger for more enlightenment is what helps us alchemise our base energy into pure golden light.

All chakras are of equal importance. Without one of them functioning correctly, the whole framework is jeopardised. The 3rd dimensional chakras are concerned with the body, the 4th dimensional chakras are connected to the mind and heart, they are also connected to development and awareness, and the 5th dimensional chakras are designed to elevate soul awareness and spiritual consciousness.

We are multi-dimensional beings, experiencing a temporary life of illusion. We are currently experiencing a life of sensory participation, a rollercoaster of circumstances where nothing is by chance, everything is carefully organised and structured so that our souls have the right opportunities at exactly the right time, to exert through free will, and spontaneity, the option to ascend, or not.

We all have the option to evolve through inner alchemy to the higher realms of existence, to the higher realms of consciousness.

These higher realms are intertwined within our 3rd dimension. We can access them through altered states of consciousness, preferably through meditation.

There are many mind altering substances, rituals, and herbs available. Being dependant on external stimulus is not as empowering as being patient and using inner alchemy.

Inner alchemy is always there within us, and comes free from any unknown, or unwanted side-effects. It is also without cost financially.

Using 'short-cut' techniques can be likened to breaking down a locked door with a sledge hammer, as opposed to using a key. Both methods open the door. One damages or destroys the door in order to gain access and the other is gentle and effective, leaving the door intact to do its job.

Our Conscious Thought Awareness is strengthened as a necessary part of the Ascension process.

In order to assist with this evolutionary thought phenomenon we can meditate and assimilate to the virtues of the affirmations associated with each of the 22 Chakras ranging from the 3rd dimension through the 4th dimension and on to the 5th dimension:

The Affirmations of the 22 Chakra System

3rd DIMENSIONAL CHAKRAS
1. ROOT I AM SAFE I trust the process of life. I am safe.
2. SACRAL I AM CREATIVE I am in perfect balance with life.
3. SOLAR I AM STRONG I see positivity and joy everywhere.
4. HEART I AM LOVED I feel my heart is full of love.
5. THROAT I AM EXPRESSIVE I express myself freely and joyously.
6. THIRD EYE I AM CONNECTED I see the future as bright and promising.
7. CROWN I AM DIVINE I know I am safe, I know I am free.

4th DIMENSIONAL CHAKRAS
8. EARTH STAR I AM AT PEACE I am open to the Great Mystery of Life
9. HIGHER HEART I AM DISCERNING I stand in my truth with strength.
10. ALTA MAJOR I AM WILLING I release all fear. I am at peace with myself
11. CAUSAL I AM MINDFUL I release all burdens. I cherish my insight
12. SOUL STAR I AM ETERNAL I accept my journey is always beginning
13. SPIRIT STAR I AM COMPLETE I am at peace with who I am
14. COSMIC STAR I AM HUMBLE I relax and accept all that exists

15. STELLA GATEWAY I AM GOD I am a spark of Creation. I am God.

5th DIMENSIONAL CHAKRAS
16. STAR CHILD I ACCEPT I am a loving child of the Universe.
17. SOLAR STAR I EXPAND I am more than I experience
18. GALACTIC STAR I BELONG I belong to everything, everywhere, always
19. UNIVERSAL MOTHER I RISE UP I love and I am loved. I create experience
20. UNIVERSAL FATHER I COMFORT I love and I am loved. I protect creation
21. UNIVERSAL SUN I SHINE I am safe in the Light. I am the Light
22. DIVINE GATEWAY ONENESS I surrender myself

Each and everyone of us is unique. When it comes to the 5th dimension and higher, we experience the new consciousness in our own individual way.

We can all share the same techniques of course, but it is our own responsibility to make the effort to develop, or not.

It is our own unique experience at every level that enlightens our psyche, allowing us to develop.

Whereas the 3rd and 4th dimensional chakras had a common physical and auric quality and purpose, the higher chakras are vortexes of divine light that will respond according to our individuality, according to our level of ascension.

Before we embark on a meditation to link us to the 5th dimensional chakras, let us take a look at the Higher Transcendental Realms of Reality. These are the realms of reality that we will embrace as we ascend.

Higher Transcendental Realms Of Reality

1. The Physical Plane
Comprising all that is matter, the lowest densest level of existence.

2. The Etheric Plane
Strongly connected to the Physical Plane, and the level we use to connect to higher planes, our own Higher Selves, and The Divine.

3. The Astral Plane
We can connect with this level through the Etheric Plane. This is where our consciousness resides after our physical body dies. As we become fully attuned to the Astral Consciousness, our consciousness ascends to the next level.

4. The Causal Plane (aka The Mental Plane)
This is where "Our Thoughts Become Our Reality". It is where the energy of our human consciousness works as thought energy. At this stage it is not working with out physical brain or body, it is working with it's own energy in it's own domain.

5. The Spiritual Plane
This is where many different levels of spiritual beings exist. They are more enlightened and advanced than we mortals.

6. The Divine Plane
On the Divine Plane, our souls can open to conscious communication with The
Divine Creator, and receive knowledge about the nature of reality.

7. The Monadic Plane (aka The Logoic Plane)
This is the Highest Plane. The level of Total Oneness. It is the level of "I am".
This is where the Holy Spirit exists.

The Seven Transcendental Realms of Reality resonate on different vibrational frequencies. Everything is energy and everything is in a constant state of motion, impermanence and transition.

The Etheric Plane is extremely close to the Physical Plane, only it resonates at a slightly higher frequency so that it is not visible to the naked eye. Our Aura resonates in the Etheric Plane, and many psychics can see images in our aura when we go to them for a reading or for advice.

Plants, trees, animals and humans all have an auric field and this is accessible on the etheric plane.

The Astral Plane is of deep significance to the Ascension process. The Astral Plane is a higher frequency to the two lower realms: the physical and the etheric.

The Astral Plane is where we can temporarily leave our physical body and, through the process known as Astral Travel, or Astral Projection, we can communicate with the higher realms as and when they lower their vibration to meet us there.

Astral Travel & Astral Projection

We are all able to access Astral Travel or Astral Projection. Astral Travel plays an important role in our ascension process and in aligning to our true life purpose. It is also essential in activating our crystalline DNA.

It is perfectly normal procedure which we all experience quite naturally when we are asleep. Children are particularly adept at astral travel. Since they are free from the concept of being totally earth bound at all times, and have no fear of floating outside their body to explore their surroundings, children often find it very simple to project onto the astral plane.

We may remember doing this ourselves. As we reach a certain level in our natural sleep patterns our etheric body floats out of the physical. We can drift beyond the confines of the physical building we are in and 'fly' around at the speed of light. Our subconscious thought guides us.

When we experience Astral Projection we are constantly connected to our physical body by our Silver Etheric Cord. Every one has one! It is this light energy cord that keeps us returning to our body after the Astral travel has terminated. It is a strong, silver energy-cord that can extend over any distance and connects our Physical body to our Astral body.

Often times, we may be able to actually see the cord when we are out of body, or projecting astrally. Even if we don't see it, we can rest assured that it is always there.

Sometimes, especially as adults, when we realise we are travelling outside the physical body, we may panic. Even for a split second, the energy of fear and panic will have us snap back into our body with a jolt. The calmer we remain during an out of body experience, the more we will remember, and we will also enjoy a more blissful and peaceful experience.

The Silver Etheric Cord keeps us connected. As we grow old, the cord naturally becomes thinner, preparing us for the ultimate transition of experiencing the death of the physical body. At this time the spiritual energy does not return to the body, the silver etheric light cord is severed and the soul returns to the Light.

Our body is very finely tuned and will snap the etheric cord for us if we are about to experience a sudden or painful accident (like a car crash or plane crash).

Before impact the cord will snap and we will transcend into the Higher Realms without feeling the awful pain of impact. We will pass on peacefully.

This has been evidenced by many psychics who receive information from deceased loved ones who have passed in tragic circumstances. Often, they send messages through Psychic Mediums that they felt no pain, but just travelled through a tunnel into the light, where they were met by loved ones they had known.

When we sleep, we travel to the Astral Plane many times. Most of us have at one time or another experienced waking up with a sudden jolt. This happens because we were participating in 'Astral Projection' whilst asleep. The sudden jolt occurs when we re-enter our physical body back on the Physical Plane. Astral travel is normal when we sleep.

We can also project ourselves onto the Astral Plane deliberately when we are in a state of deep meditation or relaxation. Astral Travel is different to dreaming. When we are experiencing a lucid dream, we are aware that we are dreaming and that were able to control what happens in the dream. When we are travelling, or projecting, on the astral plane we leave our body behind.

We can tell that we are about to experience Astral Projection, or an Out of Body Experience, if we feel ourselves floating above our physical body. Sometimes we can actually sense we are flying or floating beyond the bedroom and beyond the house. We can also look around and see our physical body sleeping in the bed below.

Our Light Body, or Astral body, can project itself onto other dimensions because material objects like walls, and obstacles like time and distance, have no meaning on these levels. Whilst matter, time and distance have no meaning, other forms of reality are consistent during Astral Travel.

When we are dreaming, bizarre things occur! In our dreams we may perhaps feel we are talking with animals, or we may suddenly feel we are in public wearing no clothes!

When we are travelling on the Astral Plane, we are travelling on the Astral Plane in actuality. It is not fantasy.

Nothing bizarre will occur as it does when we a dreaming lucidly.

We remain fully aware of what is occurring during our Out of Body Experiences, although occasionally we can sometimes come back with very little recollection, perhaps just an overall feeling of bliss, and contentment.

Often, during Astral Travel, we are able to actually witness something as it is occurring on another Continent, on the other side of the World, since time and distance have no influence on the esoteric spiritual planes of existence.

When we later learn that the occurrence was an actuality, we may otherwise be baffled as to how we knew what had occurred. It was viewed by us. It was witnessed during Astral Projection, during our Out of Body travels.

Near Death Experiences

Near death experiences are quite commonplace and many people come back from them altered and more spiritually aware individuals. Most often times, they feel themselves leaving their body, floating above it, aware that they are 'dying'.

This is a common phenomenon during surgery. The patient often finds themselves out of body, drawn to the higher light and looking down at their lifeless body undergoing medical surgery.

They also often sense positive emotions of peace as they enter a tunnel, being drawn upwards, towards a bright welcoming light. Generally they see departed loved ones, and beings of Light dressed in white, who come greet them, and to guide them. They also experience an overwhelming feeling of bliss, of pure unconditional love.

Many of us who have encountered 'near death' and out of body experiences, will vividly remember the wonderful feeling of total bliss, of pure unconditional love, for the rest of our lives. It is often an extremely personal emotional experience, and usually evokes great passion, and often tears, when recalled.

People who have experienced near death, also frequently 'see their life flash before their eyes', as they receive a Life Review.

Another common factor is the reluctance on their part, to return to the material plane; to return to their body on Earth.

Hand in hand with this feeling is the response of their loved ones and spirit guides who generally say: 'It's not your time yet."

As they are guided back to their body, they feeling a sinking down, as they reunite with their heavy physical body. Quite often they relate the discomfort of feeling the damp, warm heaviness of becoming one with their body of flesh again.

Having returned, their lives often take on a greater, more purposeful meaning, they appreciate life more, and have a greater appreciation and compassion for others.

Their lives become more mindful and they have a greater sense of self-acceptance and an elevated awareness of their own spirituality.

Generally, most people remember their near death experience as a wonderful confirmation that life is eternal, as they have been given a glimpse of the afterlife.

As we evolve spiritually, and learn travel to higher spiritual realms through mediation, we are better able to transcend the denser lower planes of existence. An individual who has little or no spiritual awareness, is more likely to project astrally onto the lower realms of existence.

The Etheric Plane is closely connected to the Material Plane, and many lost discarnate beings linger there, refusing to 'see the Light'. They still hunger for base emotional cravings, of possession and attachment; refusing to let go and trust the higher process that is within their reach.

If we resonate with the vibrations of attachment, fear and material possession, when we astrally project, or astral travel, we may experience darkness, and depressing and hostile energy that may surround us, instead of the beings of Light and loved ones we would be able to encounter and communicate with when we resonate with love, and compassion.

This is why it is so vitally important to develop our light body through meditation.

Through regular meditation, breath work, visualisation and positive thinking we can develop our chakras and our auric field. We become adept at protecting our auric field and also how to ground an earth our electromagnetic energy field.

Astral Travel allows us to reach higher dimensions. Through meditation and relaxation, (and of course, naturally through sleep), we can enjoy out of body experiences and venture onto the other planes of existence. The more we practice meditation, breath work, relaxation techniques and visualisations: the easier we will access the Higher Planes.

Breath Work

There are many different types of breath work.

At this particular time we are aiming to use the inflow and outflow of our breath to assist us in an inner deepening and an outer projection onto the higher realms of reality.

The first basic breath work technique is The Calming Breath. This simple yet effective technique brings us into a state of bodily connection and at the same time achieves a state of tranquility and deep relaxation, essential for the work we are embarking on.

The Calming Breath

1. Ideally, find a quiet place where you will not be interrupted. (although this technique can be used at any time and place without anyone even realising what you are doing.)

2. Without trying, become aware of your breathing.

3. Take a slow deep breath in through your nose, counting to 3 slowly.

4. Hold your breath in, counting to 3 slowly.

5. Breathe out gently through your mouth, again counting to 3 slowly.

6. Wait before inhaling, counting slowly to 3.

7. Repeat this circular breathing technique 3 times or for as long as you feel comfortable, allowing the breathing and the counting to get slower, and slower and as you begin to feel more and more relaxed, and in control.

Our body and our emotions are intrinsically entwined. When we are in 'fight or flight' mode and our stress and anxiety hormones are galloping through our veins, our breathing becomes fast and shallow, and our heart beat increases to uncomfortable levels pushing up our blood pressure as well.

We can take back control of our 'fight or flight' mode, by simply calming the rate at which we breathe. This is the key to allowing our bodies to return to normal functioning.

The slower and deeper our breathing is, the more relaxed we are. We are using the link between body and our emotions to take back control. As we breathe deeper and slower we are sending subtle messages to our inner self that it is safe to relax, that there is no immediate danger and nothing to fear. Breathing slowly brings about instant calm.

As we breathe deeper and slower we are also increasing the supply of oxygen to our entire system. We become more alert and our energy levels increase with the enhanced flow of oxygen.

Tranquil Calming Breath

1. Having mastered the above Calming Breath Technique, we now delve gently deeper.

2. Begin with the Calming Breath Technique, and continue from there without the conscious counting. Simply stop counting the breaths.

3. Breathe in through the nose, and exhale through the mouth, slowly and gently.

4. Allow the exhalation to be longer and slower than the inhalation.

5. Allow the breath to flow as slowly and as gently as it feels safe to do.

6. Release your conscious connection to your breath as you surrender to the vibrational frequencies of peace and tranquility.

7. Relax into this altered state of awareness for as long as it is comfortable.

8. Allow your intuition to bring you gently back to the present moment.

9. It is never about the duration of the exercise, it is always about the quality of the experience.

10. Wait a few moments before resuming everyday activities.

We may experience new sensations on all levels during this Tranquil Calming Breath Technique. We may experience physical, emotional, psychological and spiritual energy shifts.

These energy shifts are the intended results from this exercise. For example, whilst we are participating in the Tranquil Calming Breath Technique, we may feel a sense of euphoria in our heart and mind.

We may feel ourselves elevating, or floating above the physical realm. Sometimes we receive great waves of inspiration and clarity as our 3rd dimensional mind surrenders to higher frequencies.

On a physical level, we may experience shivers of electromagnetic energy both internally in our body and externally on our skin, hair and in our aura. These sensations may appear like a tingle, or tickle or even a breeze-like wave of energy.

We may begin to activate and open our third eye. The development of this 3rd dimensional chakra, the eye of insight and intuition is essential to the Ascension process.

Through gentle meditation, we can activate our Pineal Gland, (Our Third Eye) and open ourselves to the Higher Realms of Reality, the 5th Dimension and beyond.

Our Pineal Gland is the key to our being able to experience our Personal Divinity Within. Through it's activation we can experience the place of 'No-Time.' We can loose all sense of being and experience euphoric bliss as we begin to receive our personal insight and intuition.

The Pineal Gland may be just the size of a single grain of rice, but it has mystical and magical properties. Shaped like a pine cone, hence its name, it sits deep within our brain, (where the centre of our crown and third eye chakras meet and intersect, and balanced perfectly between the left and right hemispheres of our brain.)

This minuscule gland was understood to be so sacred by the Ancient Egyptians that they preserved it in a special container during the process of mummification. It is scientifically proven to release serotonin and melatonin that affect our sleep patterns and our seasonal functions.

This precious little gland is a portal between the physical and spiritual worlds. It is able to produce and release the chemical Dimethyltryptamine (DMT) which induces a euphoric experience, and gives a sense of complete Oneness and all knowing. Once activated we can transcend the material world and freely access other dimensions through astral projection and remote viewing.

One reason that modern society doesn't have this inner spiritual connection any longer is partially due to the fact that we are being fed a diet of sodium fluoride though our tap water. Fluoride is known to filter through the pineal gland and calcify it, rather like lime scale in the kettle. This renders the pineal gland incapable of its true function, that of balancing our hormonal responses in our body.

We need to seriously consider the quality of water we are ingesting. Many water filter do not filter out fluoride, which is also prevalent in toothpaste and dental treatment.

When we take back control of what we put into our physical body, and couple this with the purposeful practice of meditation we will witness amazing results. These steps are key to ascension and enlightenment. We cannot effectively ascend if our Third Eye is sightless, blind to the truth.

When we achieve the essential balance within, we also achieve the essential balance in our auric field giving us complete control of our senses as we begin opening ourselves safely to the higher realms of consciousness.

The guided meditation below is deliberately non-specific, in so far as it is now really about your responsibility, and your personal journey. It is your personal light frequency that will carry you in resonance with the higher dimensions, to higher evolved states of conscious awareness.

We may, at this point, also become aware that we still have some cords of attachment to release, some karmic ties, or some other dense energy that we need to work through and release. It is essential that we work on these aspects and free ourselves from the ties of the 3rd dimension.

There are many therapists who are perfectly placed to assist with this critical work, and rest assured that the right opportunity always arises at the right time. There are no coincidences, just a perfect pattern of ascension.

The most effective attitude anyone of us can have at this unique times, is that of acceptance and gratitude.

Acceptance of our self, our situation, our presence in the scheme of things.

Gratitude for the opportunities that arise to assist us in our ascension, and gratitude for all creation.

Relax and trust the process. Relax in the knowledge that our ascension is a long foretold event that cannot fail, that will not fail.

Relax and allow the Light to lift the veil to reveal your soul mission, your true calling.

The work that we are doing individually and collectively at this critical time will have a positive affect on future generations, and humanity as whole. It will also impact constructively on our planet Mother Earth.

This guided meditation may appear simpler than others, with less dialogue and direction. This is intentional as it is your inner alchemy and your Light Body that will strengthen and guide you intuitively.

This is good time to journal your experiences. Writing down your insights as you decipher the Light Codes that you encounter during your participation, will help anchor them into your psyche, bringing greater clarity and understanding.

As with every meditation, it is always about the quality of your experience, rather than the duration of the time spent. We are experiencing the Light beyond usual 3rd dimensional time. This meditation is one that calls upon our emotional awareness, and our spiritual awareness rather than focussing on the physical dimensions.

We are developing our Light Body and our Merkabah energy will come into its own role during this process.

This extremely important sacred geometric energy known as the Merkabah, constantly shields our light-frequencies, our aura, our light column and also plays vital and important part in our ascension process.

We examine the Merkabah in more detail after the following guided meditation to attune to the 5th Dimensional Chakras.

Once again, it is a good idea to record the meditation first, pausing at the sign ~

We can then relax and listen to the guided meditation without referring back to the text.

Meditation to attune to the 5th Dimensional Chakras

Finding yourself in a nice comfortable position, just relax totally, and without trying, gently become aware of your breathing ~

Notice the energy that you feel as you breathe.
Feel it entering your body.

Concentrate on that gentle sensation as it enters your nostrils.
Just allow the energy to flow gently ~

Allow the breath to flow as slowly and as gently as it feels safe to do so .

Allow the out-breath to be longer and slower than the in-breath.

Release your conscious connection to your breath as you surrender to the vibrational frequencies of peace and tranquility.

Relax into this altered state of awareness
As you breathe in this unconditional love energy you are totally aware that you too, are energy itself ~ that it flows through you every moment of every day.

Bring your awareness to your Auric Light Column
and the vastness of your Light Body
as you focus on grounding this frequency
at your Earth Star Chakra below your feet ~

know that you are Light, ~ you are Divinity Defined on Earth ~

You are safe ~ this is your true purpose ~
a Light Worker for the Greatest Good of All Life ~

and you are here ~
in this moment ~
in this place ~
on Earth

As these light waves of ascended awareness
increase your spiritual consciousness
you begin to sense your connection to everything ~

as you relax completely so you progress quite naturally.

Finding yourself drawn upwards through the expansive higher light frequencies ~
~ you feel acceptance ~ the awareness: I am a loving child of the Universe
being drawn higher as you begin to expand ~
you sense the awareness:
I am more, far more than I experience ~
and as you expand you accept that this is where you belong ~
feeling a wonderful sensation of the journey home:
I belong to everything, every where, always

as you gently feel the sensation of rising up~
I rise up ~ I love and I am loved ~
I can create ~
as you feel this wonderful unity with the loving life force~

I rise up ~ I love and I am loved ~
I can create ~ knowing that your every thought creates a
future ~ a reality ~
Your loving thoughts create a loving future
as you feel this in your heart
feeling so comfortable surrounded in the Light ~
I love and I am loved ~ and I protect creation

feeling an awareness a knowing that you are light
you are loved and you are able to protect all creation

as you now feel that your inner light now begins to shine~
Shining in the same harmonious frequency as the brighter
light frequencies above you ~
as you allow your light to shine ~ you become aware: I am
the Light ~

and as you connect to how bright your light shines ~
it harmonises with Divine Creator ~ that wonderful golden
resonance
as you truly, willingly surrender yourself.
Becoming at one.
~ returning into Oneness

feeling a wonderful expansion of your light body ~
as you begin to relax and just Be ~

and as you linger in this blissful state of euphoria
you feel comfortable and at peace ~

As your In-tuition gently brings your conscious awareness
back to your gentle breath,
the gateway to life ~ and beyond ~

gently breathing in the awareness of self ~
gently breathing out in the awareness of all creation ~

Bringing your focus back to the here and now,
and at the same time ~
maintaining an inner connection
to the light frequencies you have ignited
and anchored into your psyche.

Creative Visualisation

The guided meditation to attune to the 5th dimensional chakras is based on the metaphysical frequencies that we feel in our psyche, our mind, our body, our emotions and our spirit.

It is guiding us and attuning us to the Higher Realms, the higher dimensions that are always there, and always accessible to us.

We are pioneering the way for others to follow their own personal ascension process.

As we rise, so others rise too.

When we shine a light on something, it becomes clear, visible, true. It is the same with the higher dimensions of reality. When our light shines into them, they become clear, and true in our mind, in our emotions, in our DNA, and our psyche. Our Heart-Mind becomes harmoniously in tune with the 5th Dimension and beyond.

Creative visualisation and meditation are very similar and yet that have subtle differences. During meditation, we relax letting go of our everyday thoughts, allowing our ego to subside and be still, in an effort to experience inner peace. This inner peace often provides us with inspiration and insight, it often ignites our intuition.

A guided meditation is designed to relax our busy mind and purposefully create a sequence of thought energy to heal, to reveal, and to refresh our mindset.

Creative visualisation is when we deliberately set out to create and manifest a certain outcome, or a certain set of circumstances, like anew job, a new house, a new opportunity.

Later we look at how this technique is of great value in creating the new paradigm of living in the 5th dimension.

Heart-Mind-Harmony

Science has proven that we have more than 40,000 sensory neurons in our heart. They are literally brain-like cells that are in the heart. These Sensory Neurons in our heart can think and remember independently from our mind.

We are conditioned to see the world through our mind, but now we know we can see and communicate with the world through our Heart-Mind independently from the brain.

When we combine the Heart-Mind with the Brain-Mind we harmonise the energy of the Divine within, we begin the ascension process, the process of inner alchemy.

Our Heart-Mind is able to process information really quickly because it does not use logic, fear and ego.

Our Heart-Mind has no judgement and no ego. It just is. It is the Heart-Mind that connects us to the higher dimensions during the ascension process.

The language of the Heart-Mind is that of emotion, the same language that the Divine Creative Energy communicates with.

Our Heart-Mind can process information really quickly because it eliminates the need for logic, and ego. It also responds quickly to positive affirmations. These affirmations are potent tools, keys to changing negative patterns in our 3rd dimensional lifestyles.

When we combine our Heart-Mind and our Brain-Mind and communicate with our Subconscious-Mind extraordinary states of intuition and healing can be accessed.

This technique is so simple, and it releases 1,300 biochemical reactions, that promote health and boost the immune system.

One of the main keys to achieving ascension is through inner alchemy, by simply connecting to our Heart-Mind and resonating in the frequencies of love, and compassion.

The emotional frequencies of the guided meditation for attuning to the 5th dimensional chakras are the experiences our Heart-Mind uses to develop.

Consider the meditation to attune to the 5th dimensional chakras as a workout or as an exercise that gently develops and strengthens your Light Body, and your Heart-Mind.

Each time we enter the gently altered state of consciousness through the meditation to attune to the 5th dimensional chakras, we will experience something different.

No two experiences are ever the same, or are ever repeated exactly alike. Every thing is energy and that energy is in a constant state of impermanence, change and renewal.

This specific guided meditation technique also activates our Merkabah.

The Merkabah

When working with metaphysical energy we are aware that there is no such thing as empty space. There is no such thing as 'nothing'.

If we gaze at the space between two objects, we may perceive what appears to be emptiness, space, a void. This is the illusion!

There is always something there. There are always light particles, electromagnetic frequencies, atoms, gases like oxygen and carbon dioxide. There is a lot going on that we cannot see with our physical eyes, and science, once again has proven it to be so.

The atoms that make up all energy are 99.99% light, with a nucleus, protons, electrons, and neutrons taking up a minute amount of space within each atom.

The Merkabah is a Light Energy construction that resonates on the 5th dimension and higher.

As we become more spiritually aware and awakened, and as we practice strengthening our Light Body through simple, but effective techniques, so our Merkabah energy becomes brighter and more purposeful.

It is essentially perceived as a three-dimensional structure, with eight points. Often best described as two interconnected tetrahedrons, one pointing up and one pointing down.

The role of the Merkabah is to balance and shield our enhanced Light Body.

The Merkabah extends from our Soul Star to our Earth Star. Every Merkabah is individual and unique. The size, shape and frequency of each Merkabah is perfect for that particular individual at that particular moment in time.

The existence of the Merkabah embodies the truth that we are the connecting link from the Higher realms to the Earth realm.
We are perfectly designed to be sacred Guardians of Mother Earth, accessing and grounding the higher frequencies and light codes into her core centre. We are perfectly designed as the ideal channel to assist with the expansion of the intricate formation of the Ley Lines that energise life on Earth.

It is the ego-led experiences of the 3rd dimension that have warped our psyche and stolen our sense of purpose by moulding us into competitive, mind-controlled, detached beings who have forgotten the Truth of their purpose. Ancient civilisations were acutely aware of that purpose. The Merkabah can be traced back to ancient times and is often associated with the early Hebrew texts.

The word Merkabah is often used in these ancient texts to describe a divine chariot of light, or a throne. This ancient word can also be traced back further to Ancient Egyptian times:

Mer - Light
Ka - Spirit
Bah - Body

The ancient wisdom contained in the philosophy of the Kabbalah can also be identified as sacred geometry. The Ka being spirit, the Ba being body, we find that the Truth can be recognised as manifest in many forms.

The tetrahedron star of the Merkabah itself is basically a pyramid with a triangular base, rather like a three dimensional Star of David. The Merkabah consists of an upper and lower tetrahedron, each spinning in opposite directions and thereby creating a vortex, a balanced energy field.

Sacred Geometry

The Fibonacci sequence is one example of Sacred Geometry, and one which we can see in everyday life. The unfolding spiral of energy that forms a numerical pattern reflected in creation.

Like the unfurling leaf of a fern and the spiral coil of a snail shell, Fibonacci revealed how creation is made up of patterns of energy that repeat and recreate themselves in various forms.

The perfect ratio, or golden ratio, known as Phi equates to 1.61803 and is evidenced in all life. The great Renaissance artist, Leonardo da Vinci was aware of this sacred ratio of Phi and created the famous drawing of the 'Vitruvian Man'.

Curved spirals and spheres link up to make three-dimensional solids, that collectively form Sacred Geometry. It is the presence of Sacred Geometry that creates order in the Universe where there would otherwise be chaos.

There are five basic shapes or 'platonic solids' associated with sacred geometry:

>the cube, the tetrahedron, the icosahedron,
>the dodecahedron, the octahedron

Collectively these sacred platonic solids can be found in the Flower of Life pattern, an interlocking flower like pattern that can also be found as the principal design pattern running through our DNA.

There are additional shapes, but these five are the primary shapes. They can also be found in other sacred geometric formations like Metatron's Cube.

The philosophy of Sacred Geometry is a complete science in itself. It runs through all creation. At this stage in our study of ascension it is sufficient for us to comprehend images like the double tetrahedron that makes up the Merkabah Star, and to know that it is not flat but three-dimensional with four points in each of the two pyramid shapes, making eight points in total.

The tetrahedron shape is comprised of four triangles giving it great stability and balance.

These four triangular sides that make up the tetrahedron 'pyramid', ensure that it is always stable, always able to create a vortex of unshakable balance.

Since triangles are the strongest shape, four joined together in a pyramid shape, mean that it is always stable, always strong.

The tetrahedron is linked to the energy of the solar plexus, keeping the energy there grounded and also ready to rise. This is the structure that, when activated and attuned to, will protect our personal power.

The Merkabah is made of two tetrahedrons, the lower one pointing down, and the top one pointing up. They both extend from our Soul Star to our Earth Star, and create grounding vortexes of protection especially at our Heart chakra and the minor chakras on our knees.

The lower has a masculine, yang forcefield, and the top tetrahedron is energetically feminine and yin.

The upper pyramid known as the Solar tetrahedron is connected to the Higher Realms and rotates clockwise, and the lower pyramid represents Earth and is known as the Earth tetrahedron and rotates counter-clockwise.

As they rotate in opposite directions, so they bring balance and harmony to the opposite energies in our psyche:

light/dark   yin/yang   masculine/feminine
fast/slow   inhale/exhale   hot/cold

The opposing energy forcefields are coming together to create a frequency of harmony and protection. This energy interacts with our physical body, our astral body and our emotional and mental body.

The opposing directions that these tetrahedrons spin in, create an energy vortex that could be described as a 'vehicle' or 'chariot of light.'

This Chariot of Light Energy can carry our consciousness, and our Light Body safely and swiftly up to the Higher Dimensions via the Astral Plane and beyond.

The supernatural qualities of the activated Merkabah can work wonders as we move beyond the limitations of the 3rd dimensional reality. We can now access and understand the truth of the illusion of time, matter, and space.

The Merkabah shape is found in everything. It is found microscopically in the construction of our cells, plants, animals and even water.

The Merkabah itself resonates as a large single frequency in our Light Column. It is designed specifically to assist our ascension. As the lower tetrahedron keeps us connected to the Earth, and keeps us grounded during our Astral Travelling, so the upper tetrahedron carries our consciousness upward to the realms of Divine Consciousness.

The counter rotation of the pyramids in the Merkabah, and the positive force-field it produces, can activate our chakras especially our Third Eye, the eye of insight and intuition.

It is through the activation of this vital chakra that we are able to raise our Consciousness and our inner awareness.

When we combine holistic breathing techniques whilst bringing an awareness of the presence of the Merkabah star energy in our psyche, we have access to a great healing frequency.

The activation of the 4th and 5th Dimensional Chakras works in perfect synchronisation with the activation of the Merkabah Star.

Our Heart-Mind becomes more prominent in our every day living as we begin the process of ascension.

New pathways of spiritual growth and an enhancement of our understanding of the Truth are welcomed energies in our new consciousness.

As we become familiar with this supernatural realm, we find that we have the opportunity to create experiences. We have the chance to create any kind of reality we wish.

When activated and programmed, our Merkabah Star can support the lifestyle we wish to experience.

The Merkabah Star energy can also remove any latent negative energy blocks as its bright light frequency stimulates healing and renewal. As our vibrations rise we feel more connected, in control, aligned and at peace with our true intent and desire.

The Merkabah energy releases any fears that block our way. We become aware that there is no fear, there is no other sensation other than love and the many possibilities and opportunities that flow from frequency.

Our Merkabah activates quite naturally on its own, and each of our energy systems is unique to each of us. The following guided meditation assists in attuning to the Merkabah and to the virtues and purpose of the sacred geometry that it contains.

Meditation to Activate the Merkabah

*Begin by setting harmonious intent in the HeartMind ~
now focussing on the breath ~ feeling love and compassion in your heart ~*

*just noticing how the body is breathing all by itself ~
allowing that breathe to become slower and deeper ~*

*allowing the exhalation to be longer and slower than the inhalation ~
allowing the Heart Mind Harmony to increase ~*

*allow the Heart Mind Harmony to open to the frequencies of love, peace and tranquility ~
and now purposefully inhaling as deeply as possible through the nostrils
until the lungs are full ~
and hold ~
hold and focus on The Inner Void ~ The Re-Creation ~
The Great Mystery ~ the microcosm ~*

*hold for as long as it is comfortable ~
and then exhale through the mouth rapidly and totally ~
allow a "Ka" sound to flow if this is comfortable ~*

*and hold before inhaling again ~
hold for as long as is comfortable ~
focussing on ~ The Divine Creator ~ The Inter-Galactic Expanse ~
The Universe ~ the macrocosm ~*

inhaling once again as deeply and fully as possible ~ and holding for as long as it is comfortable ~ focus on the Inner Void ~ The Re-Creation ~ The Great Mystery ~
the microcosm ~

once again exhaling with the "Ka" sound ~ and holding for as long as it is comfortable to do so ~
focussing on ~ The Divine Creator ~ The Inter-Galactic Expanse ~
The Universe ~ the macrocosm

As this breathing technique is repeated three times, the "Ka" frequency resonates into the vibrations of the Merkabah ~

"Ka" the breath of spirit.

Sacred intent carried by the breath naturally and intuitively activates the vital light body energies with its vibration ~

Once this breathing technique has been repeated three times (and no more) ~
relax ~
relax and allow the mind and body to surrender to inner peace and tranquility ~

trust that the resonance in the Merkabah Star will guide and transport the spiritual consciousness to higher realms ~

relax and experience ~
relax and progress towards the higher frequencies that the Merkabah elevates us to ~
remain in this blissful state for as long as is comfortable ~

*knowing that time is an illusion and only exists in the 3rd dimension ~
the quality of the spiritual experience is manifest in our psyche ~*

*Naturally allow the breath to bring you back to the here and now ~
breathing in cherishing yourself
breathing out cherishing all creation ~
gently returning to the present moment ~
back to the here and now ~
fully grounded and earthed into the physical ~*

We do not necessarily need to focus on the shape or spinning of the actual merkabah in order to attune to it or to activate it.

The exact specification, size and frequency of the merkabah is essentially different and unique to each and every one of us. It is more essential to move beyond its appearance, and connect on the vibrational impact.

Each of us is genuinely unique. Our energy field carries such a vast array of information, past present and future frequencies, memories and attachments, prayers and promises. Frequencies that are ours, personally and individually ours.

Our Higher Self, and our Light Body frequencies work with each of us as unique individuals, as unique multi-dimensional beings. Relax and go with the proverbial flow!

We can bring awareness of this energy field of the Merkabah Star into any other spiritual, and healing work. For example, awareness of this Light Energy frequency can be valuable in crystal healing, reiki healing and it can also guide us into our own intuitive power, as it transports us to a whole new realm of ascended energy frequencies.

Why do we emphasis the "Ka" exhalation breath?

Our thoughts, our intent, our words are tangible energy that resonates in our DNA.

The Alkaline of our DNA flows with the same vibrations as emotional language, as speech, as sound.

Russian biophysicist and molecular biologist Pjotr Garjajev and his colleagues managed to modulate certain language-based frequency patterns onto a laser ray and with it they were able to influence the DNA frequency.

The key result of the work of these biophysicists was that Living DNA substances will always react to language-moderated frequencies. No other coding or invasive DNA manipulation is necessary.

The basic structure of DNA-Alkaline is identical to that of language, and intrinsically linked through the same ordered structures of our human languages. Basically, the words and sentences of human language can transform DNA structure and development.

To sum up the work of Pjotr Garjajev and his colleagues in a nutshell, the words and emotional frequencies of the human language will always affect the human DNA.

And so we now find that science has even been able to prove the effectiveness of the use of positive affirmations, hypnotherapy, breath work and and other language based therapies.

This scientific research also explains why it is possible for the "Ka" out breath to be able to connect us to our Merkabah frequency. Our sacred breath and our voice-vibes tangibly affect the light codes and frequencies that surround our psyche.

Other research that also backs up this phenomena of voice-activated renewal is the research into how singing and chanting can have benefits on our physical, mental and emotional body.

Singing, including chanting gives the body a vibration that increases vitality. When we partake in vocal chanting and singing, the human brain produces special chemicals that help us feel peace and joy. It also improves our blood circulation, which has a beneficial effect on the vocal chords, tonsils, and many lymph nodes, meaning it significantly boosts our immune system.

The blood circulation is improved during singing and this can spark positive brain activity. As the brain starts to work more intensely, our memory improves and any stored information becomes more readily accessible.

Our blood circulation is also rejuvenated when we sing and chant, especially in the head, and the body. It is even proven to assist improvements in the condition of our skin.

Singing and chanting can also assist healing especially of lung diseases, as it is not only an ideal form of breathing exercise, but it also promotes chest development, and good breathing, which significantly reduces symptoms and side-effects of lung diseases and impediments.

By regularly partaking in singing and chanting it has been proven that the levels of immunoglobulin-A and hydrocortisone increase in the body, which is a good sign of improved immunity. This is why many experts recommend singing or chanting for at least five minutes a day.

It is also why the Om chant, the Ka out-breath and positive affirmations (especially when sung) improve our overall wellbeing on all levels, physical, mental, emotional and spiritual.

Voice-activated breath-work assists renewal on an inner level, previously unexplained scientifically, but always accepted in spiritual teachings. It can even assist with the very core foundation of our DNA.

The Mysterious Human DNA

The scientific study of the Human DNA is a topic that would easily fill many books. It is of interest to us, in relation to our evolution. It is of interest to us because one again, science is exploring and revealing mysterious, supernatural patterns of behaviour in the human DNA.

Approximately only between 2% -10% of our DNA is being used for building proteins, for building our physical body. It is this minuscule percentage of DNA that is of interest to western researchers, and only this small percentage that is being examined and categorised. The other 90% - 98% DNA is considered "junk DNA" by scientists.

Nature never produces junk!

Everything in nature has a purpose. If an apple falls from a tree and is left on the ground to go soft, brown and mouldy, it is not junk. It provides essential nutrition for the earth and for many insects and birds. It is purposeful.

It is the same with our DNA. There is no junk DNA, just dormant DNA.

This dormant DNA contains seeds of information that are awaiting the right conditions to flourish.

Once again we can turn to science to prove what spiritually conscious people have always known.

The Russian biophysicist and molecular biologist Pjotr Garjajev and his colleagues joined forces with linguists and geneticists in a venture to explore the "junk DNA."

Their results, findings and conclusions are simply astonishing and revolutionary.

Their research concluded that our DNA is not only responsible for the construction of our body but that the 'dormant DNA' (the Junk!) also serves as essential data storage.

Wave Genetics

This discovery known as Wave Genetics led the Russian researchers to enthusiastically work on devices that were specifically designed to heal by influencing the cellular metabolism.

They discovered that by using suitably modulated radio and light frequencies it is possible to repair genetic defects.

For example, using Wave Genetics, Garjajev's research group succeeded in proving that this new scientific breakthrough could repair chromosomes that had been damaged by x-rays.

For many centuries esoteric and spiritual teachers have known that the human psyche is programmable by emotional frequencies, by language, words and thought, and that this transforms the physical body.

Wave Genetics has now scientifically proven and explained this phenomenon. The most important aspect of this science is that the frequency must be accurate. The intent must be the primary focus.

It is possible for us as individuals to connect with our DNA with the purpose of raising our frequency.

We can effectively use the research from the science of wave genetics to raise our consciousness to a higher level of development.

The dormant DNA will be activated by us each in its own individual time, and in its own unique way, allowing our Sovereign heritage to be remembered and recalled into our psyche.

Our Sovereign Heritage

What is our sovereign heritage? Why has it been forgotten or deactivated?

From the evidence in the earlier chapters of this book, we can deduce that mankind has risen in the past and formed well-organised, highly developed technological civilisations.
These ancient civilisations have all been long lost, their knowledge forgotten.

Yet these civilisations foretold of the present moment we are experiencing here on earth:

The Golden Age of Aquarius.
An Age of Enlightenment and Ascension.

Much of the knowledge acquired by these long lose civilisations lies dormant in our DNA.

As we ascend and raise our conscious awareness, our DNA will alter accordingly. We will not only have information downloads through re-activated light codes, we will also perfect hyper-communication skills.

This will occur when our dormant DNA, our carbon-based DNA becomes crystalline. The pressure and stress that we as a species have been put under for the past two and half thousand years, during the ego-desire-led 3rd Dimensional times, has been for a purpose.

That purpose is to pressurise us into action. When the darkest form of carbon, coal is pressurised, it transforms into Diamond.

Our inner alchemy is transforming our dormant DNA. With hyper-communication skills we will establish union, and dialogue, with higher realms, we will decipher the dormant DNA into light codes of information. This is our sovereign heritage, the remembrance that we are Divine. We are each and every one of us Divinity Defined on Earth. God incarnate. Co-creators able to bring Heaven to Earth.

If this sound superficial or fanciful lets return to the scientific field for additional evidence.

Perception and the DNA Phantom Effect

Further research by Garjajev and his colleague Poppin, resulted in the discovery of a supernatural phenomenon called the DNA Phantom Effect. This involved further scientific DNA experiments carried out on light particles (photons).

The results from these experiments concluded that we are not only multi-dimensional beings, we are also charged with the ability to create our own future.

We are co-creators of our reality. We are God incarnate.

Everything is energy. Energy is comprised of photons, Light Particles that resonate on different frequencies.

Everything is energy, and energy can be transformed as it is always in a state of impermanence and change.

We understand that both negative and positive experiences are down to personal perception. Two individuals may experience the exact same event, and perceive it in completely different ways. Perception is key to establishing our reality.

Meditation techniques can clear away artificial thought patterns, replacing them with genuine organic thoughts such as : Stillness - Focus - Bliss.

Each time someone tries something new they become a pioneer, paving the way for others to follow the same route.

They become a facilitator. As others attempt to experience the same new technique, it becomes easier and easier. This is why we no longer need to seek out a lifetime of solitude and reflection in a monastic retreat as the Gurus and Mystics of ancient times resorted to in order to achieve enlightenment.

We have progressed rapidly over generations of time, and the original advanced thought patterns that the Ancient Mystics first experienced and mastered have become engrained in our Collective Consciousness and our DNA.

Once again we can look to science to prove this.

Our whole world is made of Photons. Garjajev and his colleagues carried out further DNA experiments on light particles (photons). Photons were placed in a vacuum and were observed to be randomly scattered.

As DNA particles were introduced into the vacuum, the photons rearranged themselves around the DNA. Thus proving that DNA effected the photons. It proved that human DNA creates its environment according to its frequency.

This was an important experiment as is went against all the known laws of physics. Even when the DNA was removed the photons remained ordered. Thus proving that this manifestation works beyond the 3rd dimensional restrictions of time and space.

What mysterious force held the photons in place when the DNA was removed?

The experiment was called the DNA Phantom Effect. It showed the direct relationship between Physical World and our DNA.

Furthermore in 1990 US Army conducted an experiment to see if emotions effected living cells, especially DNA - when the cells are no longer part of the body i.e. tissue samples.

In 1993 results showed that there was an indisputable link between DNA and emotions, even following separation.

A tissue swab of DNA from the mouths of volunteers was taken and the sample was isolated. Another sample was taken and placed in an entirely different room.

In a specially designed chamber DNA was measured electronically to see if it responded to the emotion of the person it came from. The volunteer/donor was several hundred feet away in another room.

The volunteer was shown several video images designed to create genuine emotional responses: ranging from erotic images to graphic wartime footage to comedy.

Amazingly as the donor's emotions transitioned from one spectrum to another at the exact same time, the DNA particles showed powerful electrical responses.

A further experiment with a distance of 350 miles had the same results, thus proving that we are all connected, and our thoughts and our emotions are the energies that create our reality.

Everything is energy and that energy is connected. We are all intrinsically linked. This knowledge can assist us greatly in our evolution, in our ascension process.

When we are connected and influenced through positive thought and meditation, we find spiritual consciousness easier to attain.

Furthermore, the Russian scientists also found out that our DNA can cause certain vortexes in the vacuum. These vortexes science called magnetised wormholes!

These wormholes are tunnel-like connections between entirely different areas in the Universe. The purpose of these wormholes is to transmit information beyond and outside of all space and time. The DNA attracts these bits of information and passes them on to our consciousness.

Thus science has proven the phenomenon known as Hyper-communication ! Our vibrational frequency has created the energies of matter. Our vibrational frequency has impacted energetically on the 2nd Dimensional reality and created physical matter, physical reality that will elevate and permeate 3rd Dimensional in an earthly form for us to experience. Our dormant DNA once activated will impact hyper-communication with higher realms, and inter-galactic intelligence ascending to the 5th dimension and beyond.

This same scientific research directly or indirectly explains phenomena such as clairvoyance, intuition, spontaneous and remote acts of healing, self healing, affirmation techniques, unusual light/auras, the mind's influence on weather patterns and much more.

All this little-publicised scientific research proves beyond doubt our ascension process.

These facts, and this knowledge, can assist in the establishing of a new paradigm.

Hyper-communication

Hyper-communication is a phenomenon identified in the above paragraphs that has been proven beyond doubt by science.

It is activated in our dormant DNA where light codes carry information that our individual Heart/Minds connect to on an intuitive dimension. It is there that we are able to create a network of co-operation that assists our species as a whole.

As humanity experienced the 3rd dimensional reality, in order for our ego to develop and for us to experience individuality, we humans went through a veil of forgetfulness. We, as a species, lost our hyper-communication skills almost entirely.

Stress, anxiety or a highly active intellect, prevent hyper-communication being successful. Any information being channelled or received when this hyper-communication is distorted may be inaccurate and ineffective.

During the past when ego was in the driving seat, humanity rarely experienced hyper-communication. Hyper-communication can be recognised more simply as intuition.

Healers, psychics and mediums had re-acquired this phenomenon to some degree. What we are about to witness, in the very near future, are the practical impacts Hyper-communication will have on society as we enter 5th Dimensional reality.

Hyper-communication has been in action in nature where it has successfully applied itself for millions of years.

For example, when a queen ant is spatially separated from her colony, building still continues fervently and according to plan. If the queen is killed, however, all work in the colony stops. No ant knows what to do. The hyper-communication has been disrupted.

Apparently the queen sends the "building plans" even from far away via the group consciousness of her subjects. She can be as far away as she wants, as long as she is alive.

In our modern society human hyper-communication is most often encountered when one suddenly gains access to information that is outside one's knowledge base.

For example the process of channelling certain new healing techniques like crystal healing, and working with metaphysical energies like ley lines, can be considered a form of Hyper-communication. Accessing the Akashic records and past life regression therapy can also be categorised as the same hyper-communication skill.

Such hyper-communication is often simply referred to as inspiration or intuition. We will experience this in a far more meaningful way as we ascend. We will be able to communicate beyond limitation. We will be able to access information from Higher Realms for our greatest good.

Humanity is awakening rapidly. When we are consciously resonating in a unified and harmonious state in our individual consciousness, we can create a new form of group consciousness. As this new group consciousness awareness flourishes it will create an elevated dimensional frequency which will in turn give us access to all knowledge via our currently dormant DNA.

This is our Divine Right, our Sovereign Heritage. The right of free access to all universal knowledge, without restriction and without control.

Our Sovereign Heritage will lift us above the former veil of limitation and restriction experienced in the 3rd dimension. We will be on a parr with inter-galactic wisdom and new technological advances will be made without inflicting suffering and ecocide.

What is holding us back?

Why has it taken us so long?

Why has suffering been so painful and so tedious?

Commitment to the Heart/Mind Harmony

The human heart emanates five thousand times stronger electro-magnetically than the mind. The research of the Heart Math Institute has proven this. Why is it then that we as a species have not yet totally broken free from the shackles of the third dimension? Why are we so tied to the past, and past traumas?

The answer is the fact that our Ego has too strong a hold over us, and we have become complicit and compliant in our own subjugation. It is as if we have given away the control of our minds.

At the present moment we are generally guilty of living our lives distracted from the wisdom and grace of the heart.

Since heart coherence forms the foundation of crystalline consciousness, one of the main ways of making this transition easily is to simply make a profound commitment to the Heart/Mind.

Establishing a pure intentional commitment early on in our journey gives us a focal point to a moment of transitional progress.

Each and every one of us will make our pledge, our commitment in our own unique way. Remember we are all free spirits, free and individual souls, who are now ascending and reconnecting on a Higher Divine Frequency.

As we make a pledge or allegiance to honour our Heart/Mind Harmony, so we begin to release the addictive tendency to overthink and stress about daily event. So we release all lower frequency of fear, greed, judgement and hatred.

We begin to become more present and mindful of each and every wonderful moment.

As we attune to and follow the guidance from our HeartMind so we progressively replace judgmental internalised indoctrination with the voice of the compassion. We discover authenticity, integrity, inner peace and ultimately freedom.

Self-love and Self-Approval

Balancing the Yin/Yang, the Masculine-Feminine polarities within our psyche is essential to our ascension. Releasing any blocked emotions, and traumas are the essential keys to unlocking humanity's potential for evolution into crystalline consciousness.

When we process and release blocked energies, the habitual patterns of self-judgment, self-denial, rejection, victimisation and abandonment, that have only served the illusion of separation, are gradually replaced with practices of self-love, self-forgiveness, self-approval and self-compassion. As we flow with an unceasing frequency of self-responsibility, and self-commitment, our Heart/Mind Harmony shines with integrity, appreciation and gratitude.

As our inner relationship ascends to higher more harmonious vibrations, we naturally experience the sensation of self-respect. And this gradually leads to the recognition of our true Self as being Love.

"My Heart is full of Love"
"I am a miracle and I love who I am"
"I am Love."
"I am God"
"I am"

These affirmations are powerful in our ascension process. There is no separation.

When our true balance and hyper-communication are restored, star-gates, or portals, open in our heart and in our body that facilitate an instant access to multi-dimensional awareness.

We organically merge into and flow as One Universal Love.

Releasing the Past and Purifying the Present

Purification of our psyche by clearing and healing all past life trauma and ancestral patterns, is necessary in order for our ascension to higher dimensions.

Once purified our body is free enough and strong enough to enable our auric energy to download and process the higher crystalline frequencies. The resultant transfiguration enables conscious alignment with our Higher Self and our Soul's wisdom.

Many of our behaviours and beliefs are unknowingly based on blocked emotions and traumas carried over from past life trauma.

This unresolved emotional trauma may block the flow of life-force energy at a cellular level in the mind, and in the body.

Blocked energy, unresolved trauma, and unwanted cords of attachment to a person, place or event, are all discordant energies that always result in dis-ease.

As we process and release karmic ties, and past life attachments, we also expand our capacity for Heart/Mind Harmony. When we resonate in Heart/Mind Harmony our body begins to heal.

As we clear all barriers of limitation, the life-force energy connection is restored, thus enabling access to our our Higher Self, and Higher Realms of reality. As Hyper-communication is achieved and expanded, we find we have access to an almost supernatural wisdom that unifies our species as One.

This evolution clears a path for crystalline DNA to come into full expression in the body.

We effectively shift into a heart-based, body-based reality that is fluid and fully focussed in the moment. we are able to easily merge into greater multidimensional fields.

As we consciously begin to live in a multidimensional state, free from limitation and ego, totally in resonance with Heart/Mind Harmony, we ascend.

We become One, we become Divinity defined on Earth. We ascend to crystalline consciousness.

As individual Heart/Minds begin to be developed, we will find Hyper-communication becomes more acceptable too as we open to greater cosmic consciousness.

The so called junk DNA as identified by scientists, and also now re-defined by the same as dormant DNA, the 90%-98% of our DNA is about to be enlightened. Literally.

It will become transparent that we have been living up until now, in a dimension of extreme limitation. Our physical bodies limited since we only perceive 1% of the light spectrum, we cannot perceive ultra violet light or infra red light. We only see a tiny fraction of what is there.

A whole other 99% is going on without our being able to access it. Until now.

As our dormant DNA is activated the light codes it contains will bring back our Sovereign Heritage. We will once again, become whole, healed, perfect.

As our Crystalline DNA is activated so we as a species will ascend. At the moment we are experiencing the transition, from the old to the new. From the 3rd to the 5th dimension.

The road is rough and rugged but, as we each anchor and hold the inner light of peace and cooperation, of love and compassion, so we become the pioneers of the new dawn.

The inner work is of vital importance. Releasing the past, standing in the truth at the present moment, and activating our crystalline DNA.

Activating Crystalline DNA

Scientific researchers have established that if, and when, humans regain group consciousness, whilst also retaining their individuality, they would have a god-like power to create, alter and re-shape things on Earth.

In other words, when we re-establish hyper-communication we will be able to manifest our intent on the physical plane.

We are fully aware that humanity is collectively moving toward such a group consciousness of a new and compassionate kind. This shift in consciousness will require an upgrade to our ego-based physical structure.

This shift in consciousness will require an upgrade to our DNA in order to accommodate the new expansion of consciousness into a quantum light body. We are evolving as a species of Homo Sapiens, from Homo Erectus to Home Luminous.

We are remembering and re-creating our Multi-dimensional functionality.

Crystalline DNA originates in the non-physical or quantum realm. It is far more intelligent and far greater than a mere biological entity. It is the conductor of the Light Frequencies that will manifest on Earth through the Human race. Light codes that have been laying dormant in our DNA for thousands of years, are awakening and providing enlightenment.

The lower frequencies of the desire-ego-led 3rd Dimension are being transformed rapidly. Every thing appears to be in a state of chaos and confusion, yet from this chaos comes a new beginning, a new order, a new Golden Era.

As past trauma and outdated belief systems are healed and released, so the natural flow of unconditional love and compassion is restored in the mind, and body. This restoration will lead to an organic transformation of our dormant DNA, (the 90% -98% of our DNA).

The gradual emergence of crystalline DNA will result in the transformation of the physical body,

This underlying structural shift creates the foundation for illumined human consciousness to reside in the Light body anchored on Earth.

This is the process of ascension on the physical level. This new transformational crystalline DNA is now evolving on this planet to serve the evolutionary plan for Mother Earth.

Humans are designed to be Guardians, Custodians of Mother Earth. As she too begins her ascension into the higher dimensional frequencies, humans must anchor the light codes into her physical realms.

This was our original purpose.

A purpose long forgotten and long manipulated during the last Great Age of Pisces, the 3rd Dimensional age, when ego dominated the Earth.

We are witnessing the last frantic efforts of those in control of the mass media, and many global organisations and governments, to have us stay in the grip of fear, war, conflict, hatred so that they can feed off those lower frequencies, and continue to divide and rule.

That is all in the past now, those techniques of fear and control are weaker and weaker as we as a species begin to flow with the process of ascension.

As we as a species, begin to experience the transitional energy shifts in ever increasing waves, bringing the New Golden Age into reality. Raising the global consciousness to 5th dimensional reality, and higher.

The newly evolving, transcended human body based on compassion, co-operation and love represents a newly evolving species of human… the Homo Luminous.

Meditation To Activate Crystalline DNA & Ascension

Gently finding yourself in a comfortable position ~ free of stress and tension
and closing your eyes ~ just become aware of how your body is breathing all by itself ~
and the breath is so important ~
allowing that breath to become slower and a little more gentle ~
 breathing in and cherishing yourself ~
breathing our cherishing all life ~
as you gently now breathe in and connect to your inner being ~
thinking of the void ~ connecting to how small and tiny your physical self is ~
and as you breathe out gently ~ releasing that breath ~
thinking of the vast ~ the macrocosm ~ the intergalactic space
the connection to all life ~
breathing in cherishing yourself
breathing out cherishing all life ~
this wonderful flow ~ as you now allow the breath to become even slower
breathing in ~ and exhaling even slower
the out breath slower and slower
the exhalation even longer and slower ~

as you now find yourself floating above,
allowing everything to just melt away as you float above ~
you find yourself looking down at Mother Earth ~

*She gets smaller and smaller as you travel up your Light Column, at the speed of light ~
now looking down on Mother Earth ~
you can see the Light Columns of other Light Workers ~
and their presence is comforting ~*

*you can see, almost like a web around Mother Earth, where this light begins to connect ~
from heart to heart ~
you can see the soul star chakras ~ all joined together ~
beginning to create a complete sphere of light ~
the more of us that awaken ~ the more that light is anchored into Mother Earth ~*

*you feel a sense of tranquility and peace ~
you begin to acknowledge your true purpose ~
a light being ~*

*multi-dimensional
eternal
God
Creator
Divinity defined on Earth ~*

*allowing yourself now to just dwell in this higher realm~
you sense above you an even higher frequency~*

*as you attune to these higher realms ~
realms that exist in the 9th dimension and beyond ~
beyond the 12th dimension ~
higher frequencies ~
ascended masters ~
inter-galactic light workers ~*

their wisdom and love radiating down to you now ~
they have so much admiration for your progress on the Earth Plane ~
the most difficult realm of all in the Cosmos at this particular moment ~

feeling your heart gently expanding with enlightenment ~
as you feel the presence of Angels and Ascended Masters ~

these higher frequencies are so pleased and so proud that you are
standing and shinning in your truth ~

as you resonate on this high frequency ~
transported here os quickly by your merkabah ~
protected by your light column ~
you become aware of your true purpose ~

as a spark of Divine Creator ~
the light codes in your DNA begin to open ~ and shine ~
downloading wonderful information that has been long forgotten ~

these light codes, this information ~ is your divine Heritage as Co-Creator ~

and the time is right now for you to receive this information ~
and knowing that when you return to the Earth plane ~
it will become revealed to you ~
downloaded intuitively ~

as you feel the loving presence of the higher light frequencies ~
the soft petals of your heart open ~

activating the crystalline light codes in your dormant DNA ~
bringing intuition ~ information ~ and insight
deep within you ~ within every fibre of your being ~

knowing that these will be decoded and deciphered at the right moment ~
the perfect moment ~

as you now become aware of your light column ~
looking down once again at Mother Earth ~
noticing how the other light around you ~

connecting to the other spirits ~
connecting to the other versions of you ~
the other versions of creator ~

there is no separation
there has only ever been light ~

there is no fear
there has only ever been love ~
oneness ~ compassion ~
as you now float down towards the Earth Plane ~
you find yourself quite rapidly back in your body ~

still calm ~ still at peace ~
still in a wonderful relaxed zone ~
as you now begin to visualise the future ~

seeing the Earth vibrant ~
no shadows of corruption ~
just light ~

you can greet fellow people heart to heart
light to light~

its safe to walk around every day without a shield protecting your heart ~
because as you meet others ~
their love-frequency feeds yours ~ as yours feeds theirs ~

and you rise further ~ ascending in love ~

the perfect day in the future ~
there is always more than enough ~

every question, every curiosity and every need ~ is met with this wonderful way of communicating ~
we can communicate with trees ~ plants ~ birds ~ all animals ~

noticing how you visualise the perfect day ~

noticing how Mother Earth is so abundant ~
and how now the frequencies around her are helping her ~
not hindering ~
how we have all become aware of our true purpose ~
as custodians ~ guardians ~ anchors of the light code ~
creating and experiencing Heaven on Earth ~

just noticing any other information that is being downloaded and received
in your newly expanded consciousness ~

knowing that this new light is always growing and expanding within ~

and this new light is always there within you ~

*you have no fear as you stand in your truth ~
radiating light ~*

*as we now prepare to come back to the here and now ~
knowing that it is not yet quite pertinent not to shield this inner light ~
we visualise a golden eggshell-shape of protection around our aura ~*

*you might notice that your aura seems more expanded than usual
and that is how it should be ~*

*allow that golden eggshell-shape of protection to manifest now ~
grounding your energy through your earth star ~
with a constant connection to Creator ~*

*allow yourself to resonate with happiness ~
as you become aware of your new inner knowledge ~
your new intuition and insight ~*

*breathing in and cherishing yourself ~
breathing out and cherishing all creation ~*

*breathing in and cherishing yourself ~
breathing out and cherishing all creation ~*

*just as the sun shines on everything ~
without any discrimination ~
the sun just shines ~*

*so as we exhale we bless and send light without judgement ~
and this is how the forces of less-light will eventually become enlightened ~*

*as pioneers ~ as light workers ~
we are so privileged to be in this place ~
in this moment ~
with this knowledge ~*

*once again ~ breathing in ~ cherishing yourself ~
breathing out ~ cherishing all creation ~*

*gently bringing awareness back to the here and now ~
and when you're ready open your eyes and smile!*

What Will Life To Be Like in the 5th Dimension?

As we begin the ascension process, we can expect certain things to occur. Some of us will already find we can tick off some of these situations,

They will certainly all happen. They will, of course, occur at different times and in different ways, as we are all in unique situations.

We can, and will experience most if not all of the following changes in our lives.

We will find ourselves working in a more suitable job. Most likely this new work will be more like a vocation as it will most likely be connected to our true passion in life. For example, we may quit working in the corporate world and find ourselves working in horticulture, or with animals. We may leave working regular hours at a supermarket or bank for example, and begin a catering business or a building enterprise, whatever and wherever our ascended passion takes us.

Each of us will experience profound life changes. These changes will seem to just come out of the blue, since they are being perfectly channelled to us for our highest good.

We may find we retire from the world of work early and look for a sustainable, off-grid lifestyle that will, most likely involve joining forces with others to establish a community. The pooling of financial resources, alongside specific skills will be the new norm. Cooperation and compassion become the natural ground rules for our new society as it emerges.

We will find that we experience a great sense of security, as we give up worrying. Our mindset will suddenly shift away from anything that is fear-based. The frequency of fear and worry will appear to be quite alien to us. The news media channels will cease to exist as we know them today, as fear and illusion have dissolved into oblivion, no longer recognisable to our highly developed psyche.

We are also very likely to accept abundance in all walks of life. We will find we have more time for the things we love, more funds to afford our desires, and more energy in which to enjoy these things. Ascension into the 5th dimension and beyond brings our psychic and sixth senses into play. We communicate with nature and respect all creation.

As our frequency alters, so we will attract new partners, and a new friends. These new relationships will be heart based and free from the old karmic ties that have now been released. Our go-to mindset is that of our Heart/Mind, not our ego. As we begin to live in the loving vibrations of our Heart/Mind, we create a greater connection to Creator, and we experience a greater awareness of our higher purpose, as Guardians of all that exists.

Our lives begin to take on a new meaning. We no longer have a desire to meddle in the journey of others, and we no longer want to try and make things happen. We accept and we allow. We accept others for their uniqueness and allow them their freedom experience life as they choose.

We also begin to realise that there is no right or wrong, there is no good or bad. Our lives move gently forwards as we completely let go of all judgement and resonate on the frequencies of acceptance, tolerance and peace.

We know, without any shadow of doubt, that all our needs will always be met. There is no longer any need for us to stress and worry about attaining material wealth, as the class system melts away. We are all unique sparks of divine light, not classified as middle class, working class or lower class.

As we ascend as a species, as we resonate with the new golden age, we simply accept that what is right for us occurs at the right time, in the right place, and in the right way. Our understanding of divine timing becomes perfected, anticipated and accepted.

It goes without saying that living in these 5th Dimensional frequencies, our health will be improved. As we have eliminated stress, anxiety, old negative thought patterns we release main the causes of dis-ease.

We become aware that everything is energy and that all energy is light. We understand that there is no dark. There is just less light. Everything is energy and energy is light. There is no separation.

As we live our life in the virtuous energies of the 5th dimension we may find that we loose the desire to seek information through old conventional ways, like research, reading, internet searches, etc.,. As we perfect hyper-communication we know that we have access to all information.

As we activate our Crystalline DNA and our light codes in turn illuminate and inspire our Sovereign Heritage becomes paramount as we learn to use our In-tuition in resolving our curiosity.

We can expect our every need to be met in the new Golden Age. We can expect to receive every answer to every problem, and every question.

We can expect abundance on every level.

We can also expect miracles. We will become used to our every thought, wish and desire becoming manifest provided it is of the correct frequency, that of love, compassion for the greater good of all.

As we progress as a species in these higher dimensions, we will seek simplicity in all things. Our lifestyles will be less burdened by the quest to attain more and more material possessions. We will have less pressure to conform to unrealistic expectations that were common in the ego-based 3rd Dimension. Financial debt, credit cards, mortgages, and loan-repayments will all become something of the distant past.

Our psyche and our souls will find great relief as we abandon attachments to old out-dated so-called responsibilities. We will adopt a more leisurely pace to life, being mindful and savouring each moment as precious. Holding each moment as a perfect moment in time.

All these virtues and attributes, and more, will be experienced by humankind, as we purify our energy through inner alchemy. We will become more telepathic, through hyper-communication and better able to interact with other cosmic intelligence via the Astral Plane, where there is no space/time illusion.

Some of us may have already experienced some of these dynamic energy shifts. Certainly, we will all find we have a deeper compassion for all life. We will all become more creative and find a zest for life that has been denied to us for too long.

Our energies will become more tranquil and loving. As we embrace these wondrous energies, we find that nothing seems to upset us as it may have done before in the old 3rd dimension.

We will find ourselves functioning from our Heart/Mind and that we will be shielded from all negativity. Former stressful situations and anxiety triggers, that may be being played out around us, will now have little, or no impact on us at all. Where once we may have been drawn into an argument, or felt the energies of a confrontation, we now find these energies have no impact on our psyche at all. We have ascended to a higher energetic frequency.

We will find that we rejoice and celebrate more. We embrace laughter and happiness in every moment. We are hard-wired for laughter and fun, it is what our psyche enjoys most.

We will find that we no longer understand or feel the frequency of fear. We only feel the presence of peace and serenity. There is no place in our energy frequency for stress and anxiety, we only sense an overwhelming trust and acceptance that the perfect moment is here.

As we let go of the need to micro-manage our days, we trust the process, knowing that every moment of every day is the perfect moment.

We truly understand that there are no mistakes, that everything is perfectly connected and designed. We know and accept that all experiences occur at the exact right time, in the right way, and this absolute knowledge frees us from any attachments to details that would have otherwise sapped so much of our energy.

We are now free. Free from ties to the past, free from old sensations of greed, hatred, anger and fear. We have healed our inner child and it is free too. We have released all karma and negative cords of attachments to lower frequencies and we have risen as unique sparks of light energy.

How Will Our Body Cope With New Energy Shifts?

As our psyche releases old ties and blocked energies so it makes space for new incoming frequencies. As our Merkabah dynamic and the changes to our DNA occur, so we may go through a period of physical change, and there may be some accompanying minor, temporary discomfort.

We may, for example, experience aches and pains especially in the neck, shoulder and back as our Alta Major Chakra and our Merkabah evolve. The Alta Major Chakra is quite mobile between our auric field and our physical body, hence the sensations of a sudden or dull ache.

We may find that we begin to desire longer periods of seclusion and isolation. For example we may want to withdraw from social occasions on the spur of the moment, or detach from the extended or immediate family for a time. These periods of seclusion and isolation offer us the essential opportunity for inner reflection and self-assessment.

Whilst we are downloading and upgrading our ethereal, physical, mental and emotional bodies during this ascension process, we will most likely experience unusual sleep patterns. Sometimes we may find that we need very little sleep, and sometimes we may find that we need increased sleep, and even enjoy small naps throughout the day.

This is perfectly normal, as our multi-dimensional body is upgrading on all levels, and sleep is the perfect situation for assisting this vital process.

We may also notice at this time, that our dreams are more intense and vivid. Our subconscious mind is busily processing and releasing the past and this may reflect in our dreams. Past traumas, and injustices that may go back over many previous lifetimes are now being reviewed and released in order to make light our journey of ascension.

All negative energies that would otherwise weight us down are being lifted, and enlightened.

Amongst many other symptoms of ascension we may experience the feeling of being spatially challenged. For example we may feel disorientated, out of body, even though we are in familiar surroundings. A good remedy for this is to ground our frequencies by spending more time out doors in nature, perhaps gardening or walking.

As we enter the new higher frequencies of the 5th dimension we may feel a subtle sense of loss. We may miss the former passion we had for our old hobbies and habits.

But we need not worry since as we ascend in consciousness, we will find new vibrant opportunities arise that broaden our horizons, allowing us to experience a new lifestyle, a new society, a new world.

Some of us may find ourselves feeling detached from those around us. We may feel loneliness, even when we are in the company of others. This loss of passion, this desire to participate less, is a common symptom of ascending to higher consciousness.

As we begin to feel less attached to the former materialistic, desire-led, realm of the 3rd dimension, we feel an almost magnetic pull towards the new higher vibrational realms.
We realise that this higher reality is where we truly belong.

And we also realise that we agreed to be here on Earth, at this critical time.

We understand that we are not here alone, that there are many of us here and we are coming together to share our experiences and to work to anchor the incoming Light Codes that will assist humanity and Mother Earth to transition safely.

At this transitional time it is perfectly usual for us to feel out of body, and we may even begin to see or sense ourselves from our higher self perspective. Our sensitivity to our surroundings may also be heightened and this may create a sense of overwhelm especially concerning noise and crowds.

We will find we have an intolerance to old attitudes that are still engrained in the 3rd dimension.

Conversations, movies, and even groups of friends that we once found fascinating, now hold no interest to us at all. On the contrary, we feel the immediate urge to distance ourselves completely from them.

Even old routines may begin to feel wrong. Once we have glimpsed life from a higher awakened consciousness, we will have very little desire to go back.

We will find that we have a more heightened awareness of our true purpose here on Earth, that of Guardianship. We are designed to anchor the light frequencies into the Earth, later we look at how we can do this in more detail.

As we go through major changes in our chemistry and electromagnetic energies, we may find that we experience headaches, blurry vision and loss of memory. We may have heart palpitations, and mild chest discomfort as our heart chakra opens to higher levels of consciousness.

It is very possible that at this time we begin to access greater telepathic skills. As we undergo an essential de-programming, so we make room for hyper-communication, we experience deja vu, vivid dreams, and downloads of cosmic knowledge that was formerly inaccessible.

Essentially we become more discerning. We sense the truth as it resonates in our heart, rather than using logic in the brain. Old conditioned responses now leave our psyche entirely.

This transition we call Ascension is being assisted from inter-galactic entities. They are guiding us as best they can given our current situation. They are patient, and full of pride and admiration for our efforts so far on the Earth Plane, the most difficulty realm of reality in the Cosmos, at this current moment.

As we step into our truth and embrace being multi-dimensional free spirits, so we attract guides, and ascended light workers from the higher realms. We begin to realise that we are pioneering the way forward as we evolve from Homo-Sapiens to Homo-Luminous - Light Beings.

As we go through this major transition we may occasionally we feel pangs of panic and anxiety as our ego begins to lose itself. Our Ego may begin to feel vulnerable and powerless and it may present false sensations of panic and anxiety. These will be short lived, and can be remedied with the assistance of techniques we look at later.

We begin dwell more and more in our Heart/Mind we start to re-evaluate what is real. Our sense will become more evolved and we will feel emotions deeper, we will see colours with more vibrancy, we will also express ourselves in new ways as we discover new lifestyles that assist with our ascension.

Our thoughts, words and actions are now coming from our Heart/Mind. We may experience a sense of being interconnected to all life. As we have an overwhelming desire to surrender totally to the spiritual process, as we become an instrument, a channel for the Divine Creator.

The Higher forces in the advanced spiritual realms; our spirit guides, light workers, ascended masters, and angels, will assist us in this process of trust and surrender.

Trust & Surrender

As we ascend in consciousness, our ego has transformed into a passive and compliant energy that no longer resonates on selfish frequencies. It still looks out for our overall wellbeing, but it is no longer able to interject itself in a negative 3rd Dimensional way.

The willingness of our individual soul energy to surrender is entirely without pressure, and without coercion. We find that we are ready and willing. Even more than that, we are eager to trust the higher process, and to surrender every moment of every day.

This surrender frees us from bonds of attachment, from the tedium of overthinking and the burden of overwhelm.

When we surrender and trust that we are now resonating for our highest, and greatest good in every possible way, so we become a divine channel.

When we surrender Spirit openly determines how and what we experience. We find that the details of our work, the fluency of our income, the quality and variety of our experiences, are all delivered with infinite precision.

Everything happens in exactly the right order, at exactly the right time in exactly the right way for our highest good. We know this and accept it as the new norm.

Once we experience this new paradigm there is literally no going back.

Time is no longer linear, moving in one direction at one pace. It is simultaneous and we can co-exist on all levels, past, present and future.

Our perfected Merkabah energy field allows us to shift on a higher plane, beyond separation, beyond space and beyond time, as all dimensions become accessible.

As we relax, and enjoy the processes of ascension, we willingly and naturally find we have an overwhelming desire to trust and surrender. Trusting that every moment is perfect, and surrendering to the Divine Blueprint.

The Blueprint for our own individual role in the new paradigm, is intrinsically woven into the Blueprint for Mother Earth, and for all humanity.

We become aware that our role, and the role of Mother Earth, has always been interlinked.

It is time for us now to stand in that truth and manifest Heaven on Earth.

And as we do so, we become aware that nature has provided for our every need, with such vast abundance, there is always more than we can use.

Life in the new Golden Age will differ greatly from the lack and limitation of the 3rd dimensional matrix, yet some of the new infrastructure is already in place, it just needs a little tweaking. In other areas, a completely new paradigm will evolve.

Out of the ashes rises the Phoenix, out of chaos comes order, and out of the drudgery of the dark comes the luminosity of the light.

A Practical Guide to the New Matrix

We actually chose to be here at this critical moment in time, when the Earth is shifting into a new paradigm.

We chose to be here because we knew had the tenacity and strength to be of service. We chose to be here to assist with the anchoring of the intense incoming light codes. we chose to be here so that we might exude peace and tranquility whilst chaos reigned all around.

We were chosen. Chosen to be here to support the incredible energy shift that will effect the entire Universe. The new Golden Age of Aquarius now becoming manifest, and it will not fail to evolve.

We were chosen to be here to assist in this Great Cosmic Shift. We endured the old order, our inner self always knew we were more than the illusion of the old matrix, we are more than temporary human beings, we are more than the suffering and detachment that the old order taught us through its lies and deceit.

We have always sensed and known that we are Multi-dimensional beings, and that we are here to be of service. Service for the good of all creation.

Our greatest joy is rarely found in the relentless pursuit of selfish ambition. We inherently have always known we have been designed for something far greater than ourselves.

What we give to another
We give to ourselves,
We are all One

That other person, is just another version of you.

Our sacred assignment will become clearer every moment of every day as our dormant DNA becomes activated.

As we download our Sovereign Heritage and develop into the unique Co-Creator we were intended to be.

The age of deception, delusion, and detachment is over. It is not going quietly by any means, since that is its nature: deluded, deceitful, dis-eased.

The old order, the 3rd dimensional reality sought to strip away our divinity. It kept us divided and fearful.

Those old tricks just don't work anymore.

We have risen.

Creating a New Paradigm

> *"We must begin with the heart of mankind*
> *- with conscience -*
> *and the values of conscience*
> *which can only be manifested*
> *by selfless service to humanity."*
>
> Albert Einstein

A scientifically controlled study conducted by researchers at the University of Kassel have proven that wile the chest area of an average person emits 20 photons of light per second, someone who meditates on their heart centre and sends love and light to others, emit an amazing 100,000 photons per second.

That is 5,000 times more than the average human being.

Numerous studies have also shown that when these photons are infused with a loving and healing intent their frequency and vibration increases to the point where they can literally change matter, heal disease and transform negative events.

This, once again is Science technically proving what spiritual adepts have always known.

When we are operating from our Heart/Mind we can change the matrix. We can co-create a new paradigm, a new dimension.

Our heart not only loves, feels, thinks and remembers it also has the ability to communicate with other hearts. It stores information through the body. It is far more than what modern science would have us believe.

When we fully utilise our Heart/Mind in harmonious synchronicity we will have developed a group consciousness of a new kind.

The new group consciousness will be able to co-create an Earth bound realm where there would be no environmental problems nor scarcity of energy. For everything will be abundantly available to meet our every need. Every solution will be harmoniously available.

As we begin to resonate on the same frequency as one another, our Heart/Mind clarity will raise the collective consciousness.

As a unified civilisation there will be no suffering, no lack, no despair or disease.

The children of the New Golden Age will be born to live life to the fullest. They will not be born to experience suffering, fear and oppression.

The children of the New Golden Age will be born with their Sovereign Heritage in tact. They will know the extent of their uniqueness. They will be fully aware of why they are here and what they wish to experience, what they wish to contribute to the wonder of creation.

Since the base vibrations no longer exist, it is normal to greet one another heart to heart.

We will no longer need to constantly shield, ground and protect our energy field, since the new paradigm is one of love and compassion. The children of the New Golden Age will not be brain-washed into consumerism. They will experience the freedom of fully expressing their inner heart/mind, their individual light.

As the children of the New Golden Age step into their heritage here on Earth, they will be able to transcend the limitations of the old order, and communicate freely with the higher dimensions of angels, and the intelligence from inter-galactic beings.

Education in the New Golden Age

We are already witnessing a change in the way our children are being taught. Many children are traumatised by the idea of attending School as it is in the old dimension.

The old institutions will cease to operate as they previously did. Schools, playgroups, colleges and universities will all unhook from the old programming.

As our dormant DNA becomes activated we will see children living as free spirits, able to study subjects that fascinate and inspire them.

They will bring their unique talents, insights and skills with them directly to Earth, since there is no longer a veil of forgetfulness, since there is no longer any karma, as all past ties of restriction are dissolved.

We discussed earlier in this book how ancient civilisations predicted this new golden age, this transition of Earth and Humankind.

The culture of the Native American Indian understood this. They lived in relative harmony with all life, honouring all Creation. There are four philosophical points in Native American Indian culture that will become manifest in the new Paradigm.

The first philosophy states: 'The person you meet is always the right one'.

That is, no one comes into our lives by accident, all the people around us who interact with us, stand for something, either to educate us or to help us in our situation.

The second philosophy states: 'What happens is the only thing that can happen'.

Nothing that happens could have been different. Every detail of every occurrence, every moment of every day, is divinely planned: perfect in every way.

The third philosophy states: 'The moment something begins, is the perfect moment'.

Everything starts at the right time, not sooner or later. When we are ready for something new in our life, it's already there to begin with.

The fourth philosophy states: 'What's over is over'

When something ends in our life, it has served its purpose This realisation encourages us to let go and move forward without ties to the past, without guilt, without limitation.

These ancient philosophies will become the norm in the new paradigm. The education of the children of the New Golden Age will embrace these deep meaningful points with clarity and with ease.

As hyper-communication becomes integrated into our new collective consciousness we will find sitting in a classroom a thing of the past. Our newly attuned in-tuition will mean that we simply know the answer to our question. We simply understand the solution to our quandary.

New solutions and new technologies will evolve with divine timing.

And this is possible because we are no longer in a state of delusion and detachments.
In the new paradigm we are enlightened, we are divine, we are co-creator, God/Goddess.

As the new paradigm begins to manifest we will experience profound energy in all areas, mental, physical, emotional, and spiritual. There are techniques that will help us to cope during these monumental energy shifts.

Keeping A Journal

*"Hold a thought for just 17 seconds and the
Law of Attraction kicks in.
Hold a thought for 68 seconds and things move:
manifestation has begun"*
~Abraham Hicks~

Keeping a journal is often very beneficial as we can look back and re-connect with just how far our ascension journey has evolved.

Jotting down our honest innermost emotions and thoughts has a cathartic cleansing effect as it is literally pulling the thought forms out of ourselves and consigning them to being addressed in a physical form.

Whilst we are reflecting in our journals we can observe and analyse such topics as:

How does my physical body feel?
What emotions am I truly experiencing?
Where am I Spiritually?
What do I want to visualise for myself, and my loved ones?
What would I welcome for my environment and society?
What am I learning now?

We can use our Journals to visualise the future, knowing that creative visualisation techniques worked in the old 3rd dimension, and they will be even more potent and effective as we embrace the higher frequencies of the 5th dimension and beyond.

Future Energy Solutions

Visualise future energy solutions that are free from pollution, and corporate corruption.

As we ascend collectively we will download the solutions that were previously denied us.

We are already aware that Hemp and Bamboo will play essential roles in the New Earth. These two plants will rapidly rebalance much of the ecological damage that has been caused by the greed and ecocide ravaged on this beautiful planet.

Many new technologies will emerge, and solutions to highly toxic substances like radioactive Plutonium will manifest. Scientist already have some ecological solutions for our new future energy solutions, but they have been restricted by the global corporations who wish to rinse out every penny from fossil fuels, no matter what the cost to the planet.

Those days are over. The old days of raping Mother Earth with little or no regard for her sustenance and survival are unsustainable and about to become obsolete.

If we can just take a moment to see life here on Earth as our counterparts do from the higher realms. What an absolute mess humankind has made of it all.

The blessing of freewill that our ego was gifted wasn't used for the greatest good at all. Everything suffered, humans, animals, even the planet that sustains us.

Now, we are thankfully rising from this suffering and through our experiences in the 4th dimension, we are gratefully returning to our true self. With clarity, and with wisdom. With insight and intuition.

Part of our ascension process will be the great revelation of hidden truth.

Climate Change & Weather Manipulation

We understand that in the new paradigm everything will work for the highest good of all creation.

At the present moment we need only look up at the sky to witness Geo-engineering, otherwise known as weather manipulation.

The scientific world has never been so divided on any single topic as it is on this one. There are those scientists who believe it is essential for the skies to be sprayed to deflect the rays of the sun to limit global warming. And there are those scientists who feel that any intervention on this scale is far too risky.

Such radical intervention in Earth's natural rhythms, will also impact on the entire Universe. Experiments with Geo-engineering will also have unknown effects on areas of our planet that have not agreed to these trials, since everything impacts on everything else.

Cloud seeding has been in operation since 1952. Trials and experiments with cloud seeding have taken place all over the globe. Carbon capture and solar radiation management trials have also been in use for many years.

These controversial weather manipulation technologies will impact on many levels:
* the Schumann Resonance, known as Earth's heart beat, will be altered

* this alteration of the Schumann Resonance leads to mass beaching of whales, and flocks of birds loosing their orientation etc
* people have reported an increase in tinnitus, raised heart beats etc
* the seasons have been displaced and plants are struggling to adjust accordingly
* blocking the rays of the sun and deflecting them back into space will have an unknown and as yet unquantifiable impact on the cosmos.

What is the solution to this quandary?

We have all the skills at our disposal right here and right now, and right within our own psyche.

As ascended multi-dimensional beings we can come together in collective collaboration, working together to manifest the Perfection of Creation.

As we activate our Crystalline DNA, remember this is an incredible 90-98% increase in our potential. It is not just a doubling or quadrupling of our intelligence, but almost 100 fold increase.

It may be hard for us to imagine what this may feel like.

It may hard for us to imagine just what we are really capable of.

Until the ascension process begins; and then we will become aware of our True Life Purpose.

And as we rise, we no longer need geo-engineering and intervention by technology.

As we rise, we realise that we can bring about change by visualisation, by meditation, by using our new-found sovereignty as Co-Creators.

This may sound over-simplified, but that is the beauty of Ascension.

It is simple.

Positivity & Opportunity

One small positive thought first thing in the morning can change the whole day. As we sustain the force of well being we shift our energy and with it the energy of our environment.

When we have traversed the path of Ascension, our thoughts will manifest quicker and easier than ever before.

Humanity is currently at the leading edge of Thought/Consciousness. Everything is a thought first, and then a vibrational thought, and then as that is thought is thought upon longer and longer, with enough attention given to it, it takes shape, and form. All matter is vibrational interpretation.

In the new paradigm, our thoughts and intentions will be Heart/Mind based. They will be in harmony with Creator, and there will be no limit to the beauty and tranquility we can manifest on the Earth Plane.

In the past we needed to look beyond religion. So many faiths and religions held us back. We were so often lead to believe that we were here on Earth to suffer, or that we had created bad Karma and must be punished or that we were here to learn harsh lessons.

Now, as we step into our Sovereign Heritage we truly understand:

> We are the creative energy
> We are the God/Goddess
> We are the Source/Universe
> We are the Co-Creators

As we ascent we tap into the force of the Divine Creator, and we experience ourselves as part of it; not as a separate entity.

The Past is Over

The image that comes to mind of the old order is rather a comical vision, of a couple of obscenely wealthy old men, like corrupt Bond villains, (with or without their cat) who wish to control the World. This image is not as far fetched as it may seem.

In the past, as the earlier chapters in this book identified, we were ruled by narcissistic psychopaths who indeed, competed with each other to rule the World.

Their ego-led desires to out-do each other for greater power, control, wealth and gain at all costs, has almost cost us everything we hold dear.

As these out-dated forces attempt to cling to the old shadows of the past, we are likely to witness much fear-mongering, many attempts to divide and rule.

The ascended power that we now download, will counter these experiences, rendering them ineffectual and futile.

Watch and witness these tricks, these manipulations of the masses. When you see them through the eyes of an ascended soul, you will see them for what they truly are.

The Future is Written in the Stars

The Golden Age of Aquarius is long foretold by wise, ancient civilisations, now long gone.

Astrologically the planetary alignment in 2012, identified in the Ancient Mayan Calendar, ushered in this inevitable transition.

At this moment in time there are many Inter-Galactic forces focussing on what is occurring here on Earth at this moment as what happens here will inevitable impact on every part of the Cosmos.

These higher forces, operating for the collective greater good, are not going to sit idly by and allow Earth to be at the mercy of the former ego-led psychopaths.

In the past, the Earth has been manipulated and exploited and everything on the earth plane has endured suffering as a result.

We began our journey in this book with the opening phrase:

"Everything is energy, and everything is in a state of impermanence and change."

That truth is never more pertinent than now.

Everything is in a state of impermanence and everything is changing.

As we work on our inner self, as we traverse our unique inner path to Ascension, so too we inspire and affect change on a larger scale. The microcosm reflects the macrocosm.

By standing in our truth and holding the light we dispel all fear.

Without fear, we are able to stand in our truth and hold the light.

> As above so below
> As within so without

As our Crystalline DNA ignites so we intuitively know the Truth.

As our Hyper-communication skills are perfected, we transmit the Truth to all humanity.

Even those operating from the shadows of darkness, will be effected by the Light of the Truth. Even those operating from the shadows of darkness will feel the waves of Ascension lifting them ever higher towards the inevitable Golden Age.

It is prudent not to accept anything that has been genetically manipulated, genetically altered, or genetically manufactured since this may delay your Crystalline DNA activation. Nothing can prevent ascension, but it may delay it, or cause the process to be more tedious.

Look with eyes of enlightenment at where Truth resides. The throat chakra.

The throat chakra of Mother Earth is found in the Middle East, an area which has been deliberately held in fear, distrust, disruption and despair. As we hold inner peace and work towards releasing our own inner fears, so this will manifest on a global scale and release the tensions held in this vortex.

We first begin with ourselves, and then we allow the process to expand.

We have all the skills at our fingertips, and the techniques and meditations contained in this book will assist us in the process of ascension, as we co-create the new paradigm.

Meditation: Holding the Light

Finding yourself in a quiet and comfortable position, and gently closing your eyes,
notice how your body is breathing, all by itself ~

take a moment to attune to the miracle that you are ~

breathing in ~ I am
breathing out ~ at Peace
I am ~ at Peace

visualising your inner energy as ~ all Light ~
connecting to your Earth Star Chakra ~
sensing the connection to other versions of you ~
the other light-workers ~
feel the comfort of their presence ~

breathing in ~ I am
breathing our ~ at Peace
I am ~ at Peace

relaxing the breath now and surrendering to the Light as you
sense the Higher Light Frequencies above you ~

rising up ~
through your light body and light column ~
through the kaleidoscope of iridescent celestial light ~

looking down at Mother Earth ~
rising higher and higher ~
relaxing and surrendering to your Merkabah ~

as your Merkabah guides you to the perfect place ~

breathing in ~ I am
breathing out ~ at Peace
I am at Peace

looking down now and seeing the Earth as if for the first time ~
the beautiful blue waters ~
the verdant green vegetation ~
the clear fresh air ~

feeling and appreciating the miraculous creation with such wonder ~
allowing your sacred heart to open with an out pouring of pure love ~

bringing your awareness to your connection to this creation ~
bringing your awareness to the significance or your part in this creation ~
sensing and feeling your desire to protect this creation ~

as you feel the presence of the higher realms of light above and beyond you ~
the realms of the Ascended Masters, the Inter-Galactic Intelligence ~
the presence of your Spirit Guides ~ and the loving presence of Angels ~

these invincible forces for Higher Good are working with you ~
they are so proud of your achievement on the Earth Plane ~

the most difficult realm of reality at this present moment in time ~

*as your light codes download into your crystalline DNA ~
you have an overwhelming sense of connection ~
you are Light ~
you are Truth ~
you are Divine ~*

*and as you linger here a while ~
basking in the tranquility of blissful euphoria ~
you know that this is your real home ~
this is your real self ~*

*as you realise that you ~ and only you ~
can manifest this same frequency on Earth ~
you are essential to the whole process ~*

*feeling and sensing connection to everything ~
feeling and sensing love and compassion ~
feeling and sensing guidance connection to ~
and from the higher forces for greater good ~*

*breathing in ~ I am
breathing out ~ at Peace
I am at Peace ~*

*looking down at Mother Earth with eyes of enlightenment and love ~
feeling the Truth of your role on Earth ~*

*as you gently float down to re-connect with the new paradigm ~
feeling and sensing your commitment as a Light Worker ~*

Invincible ~
Eternal ~
Light ~

breathing in ~ I am
breathing out ~ at Peace

I am at Peace
~Always~

Conclusion

The writing of this book has taken a lot longer than I had first anticipated. I have rewritten the first chapter many times as circumstances and global events occurred that had been foretold in the earlier text.

Surrendering to the process, I have learnt a lot myself and I am grateful to the Higher Forces for channelling this information through me.

Once our insight is activated and we see the Truth through eyes of enlightenment and love, we cannot return to the old ways. Why would we?

Heaven on Earth awaits us as we Ascend as Multi-dimensional beings.

As the Truth of Our Sovereign Heritage downloads into our newly activated Crystalline DNA, so we will begin to utilise our new-found Hyper-Communication skills to perfect manifestation of the Higher Dimensions on the Earth Plane.

It has been a pleasure and a privilege to share the unique techniques and information that was channelled in the writing of this book.

About The Author

Teresa is recognised as a pioneer in her field as she began teaching spiritual awareness in the early 1980's, advocating the advantages of Aromatherapy, Crystal Healing and Past Life Recall at a time when these disciplines were little recognised and understood.

A registered Life Coach and Hypnotherapist she is also a Reiki Master Healer and Teacher.

www.relaxandprogress.co.uk

Printed in Great Britain
by Amazon